Generative AI for Beginners

Your Essential Guide to Artificial Intelligence: Real-World Applications to Simplify Your Life, Save Time and Navigate Ethical Impact with Confidence

Sarah T. Rowan

AF719496

Copyright © Sarah T. Rowan. 2025 - All rights reserved.

The content contained within this book may not be reproduced, duplicated or transmitted without direct written permission from the author or the publisher.

Under no circumstances will any blame or legal responsibility be held against the publisher, or author, for any damages, reparation, or monetary loss due to the information contained within this book. Either directly or indirectly. You are responsible for your own choices, actions, and results.

Legal Notice:

This book is copyright protected. This book is only for personal use. You cannot amend, distribute, sell, use, quote or paraphrase any part, or the content within this book, without the consent of the author or publisher.

Disclaimer Notice:

Please note the information contained within this document is for educational and entertainment purposes only. All effort has been executed to present accurate, up to date, and reliable, complete information. No warranties of any kind are declared or implied. Readers acknowledge that the author is not engaging in the rendering of legal, financial, medical or professional advice. The content within this book has been derived from various sources. Please consult a licensed professional before attempting any techniques outlined in this book.

By reading this document, the reader agrees that under no circumstances is the author responsible for any losses, direct or indirect, which are incurred as a result of the use of the information contained within this document, including, but not limited to, — errors, omissions, or inaccuracies.

Table of Contents

CLAIM YOUR FREE ESSENTIAL AI QUICK-START TOOLKIT NOW!

Before you dive into the transformative journey of understanding Generative AI, get equipped with your exclusive **AI Quick-Start Toolkit** to get the maximum benefits from this book. The toolkit is jam packed with invaluable resources to make AI a practical part of your everyday life.

What's Inside the Toolkit?

- **Comprehensive AI Glossary (PDF):** Understand **140+** key terms effortlessly and build a solid foundation as you progress through the book.
- **AI Prompts Cheat Sheet (PDF):** Discover **160** ready-to-use prompts for ChatGPT and other tools for you to test as we explore each domain in the book.
- **AI Tools Links Shortcut (PDF):** Keep **60+** AI tools at your fingertips with direct links, ready for you to explore as they come alive in the pages of this book.

Get Started: Download Your AI Toolkit Here

https://generativeaiforbeginners.systeme.io/freetool

Begin exploring AI today!

Introduction

Every day, the gap widens between those leveraging artificial intelligence (AI) to transform their lives and those watching from the sidelines. It's time to welcome this revolutionary tech into your life, reclaiming hours of your day, multiplying your creative output, and solving problems that once seemed insurmountable.

Like many people, I was initially unsure about AI's role in my life. I knew it existed, but I wasn't convinced it would significantly change my day-to-day activities.

That changed when I started noticing how often I was already using AI without fully realizing it. When I unlock my smartphone with facial recognition, browse personalized recommendations on my favorite streaming platform, or ask my virtual assistant for the weather forecast – AI is there, quietly making things simpler for me.

This realization sparked my curiosity. If AI was already helping me in ways I hadn't recognized, what might be possible if I intentionally learned to work with it?

I got curious and delved into articles about AI, joined online communities, and took online courses to develop these new skills properly. What really changed everything, though, was simply experimenting with different tools myself. That hands-on practice helped me confidently identify which AI solutions actually solved my specific problems. This is how I learned how to easily integrate AI into my personal and professional life – practice, trial and error.

Looking back on my learning curve, I realized what was missing: a straightforward guide that compiled all this practical knowledge in one place. That realization inspired this book – a comprehensive resource designed to help you confidently use AI tools and applications to simplify both your personal and professional life.

Let me walk you through how this book is organized, which is in four parts to guide you through AI essentials and show you how to apply these tools effectively in work and daily life.

Part I: Foundations

You will familiarize yourself with the core concepts of AI and some of the basic but essential AI terminology. You will also get clear guidance on choosing the right conversational AI tools from the growing marketplace.

Did you think there was only ChatGPT? You'll be surprised to see how many others you can consider.

In this section, I also address the many common misconceptions and concerns people often have that AI will replace human intelligence or that it's too complex for the average person to understand. Rest assured, those myths will be put into perspective with realistic expectations about what AI can and cannot do.

Part II: Practical Applications of AI in Daily Life

You'll get more hands-on and see the many uses AI has in the real world in this section, where I explore a wide range of use cases in the domains that resonate with most of us. You'll discover how to boost productivity, improve organization, manage personal finances, enhance learning, and even use AI for fitness, meal planning, and creative pursuits such as writing, music composition, and video creation.

Part III: Boost Your Confidence in Using AI

You`ll focus on mastering what you've learned so you can confidently interact with AI to troubleshoot common challenges and refine your ability to use AI tools in a natural and intuitive way. You`ll learn the ethical and societal implications of using AI to make informed decisions for using intelligent tech while keeping you and your data safe.

By that point, you will be ready to integrate AI into your professional life. Whether you want to upskill for career growth, enhance workplace collaboration, or even explore emerging AI-driven industries, you will already have a competitive edge through your ability to customize and leverage AI for specific professional challenges.

Part IV: What's Next?

You`ll get a heads up on how to stay ahead of future AI advancements. You'll also gain insights into the future of work in an AI-powered world, plus recommended resources to continue your AI learning journey.

Learning by doing is at the heart of this book. Each section includes practical exercises and real-world projects that reinforce concepts through direct application – opportunities to apply what you've learned immediately. Active engagement with these challenges is where true growth happens. Practice creates confidence.

This book is designed to be your faithful companion, to make practice easier and effortless, helping you embrace AI with confidence and engage with it on your terms.

You now know exactly where to start: just turn the page.

PART I: FOUNDATIONS

1

TAKE THE FIRST STEPS ON YOUR AI JOURNEY

I first realized how deeply embedded AI is in our routine lives when I was ordering groceries online. With a few taps on my smartphone, the app remembered my previous purchases and suggested other items I might want based on my past choices – some of which I had completely forgotten about!

The app seemed to know me better than myself. I was curious – how did it all work?

At first glance, AI appears to be a complex web of algorithms and codes, but like my personalized grocery app experience, the mysterious AI behind the scenes was merely a collection of tools that are interconnected to simplify and enhance our daily lives.

Defining AI and Debunking Myths

At its core, artificial intelligence is machine intelligence designed to mimic human cognitive functions. That doesn't mean that machines think like us. They simply process data and execute tasks in ways that resemble human reasoning.

Unlike traditional computing, which follows explicit programming instructions to perform tasks, AI systems are designed to learn, reason, and solve problems independently. They thrive on data, improve with experience, and adapt to new inputs, much like humans learning from their environment.

AI's learning ability means it can identify patterns and make decisions with minimal human intervention – a quality that sets it apart from conventional software.

But let's be really clear here about what AI is not. AI is neither sentient nor capable of emotions or independent thought. In reality, it's just a sophisticated tool that processes vast amounts of data to perform specific tasks very efficiently.

Despite its growing presence, AI's reputation often bears the brunt of myths and misconceptions – one common fallacy being a fear that AI will replace humans in all aspects of work and life. While AI can automate specific tasks and perform them with far greater speed and efficiency than us humans, without demanding a paycheck, the AI revolution is, in fact, creating a wealth of opportunities for diverse new roles that require human creativity, oversight, and ethical judgment.

Another misconception is that AI possesses human-like intelligence, leading to concerns that machines could become autonomous beings. In reality, AI lacks consciousness and only operates within the boundaries set by its programming and data, so we're not about to witness a robot rebellion any time soon.

Additionally, we may mistakenly believe that AI is synonymous with machine learning, but actually, machine learning is just one subset of AI.

There's also confusion over the relationship between AI and robotics, with assumptions that all intelligent machines are AI-driven robots. But while AI can indeed power robots, it also operates in non-physical applications such as data analytics and natural language processing.

When you recognize these distinctions, it dispels any misconceptions you may have had, and fosters a balanced view of AI as a powerful ally in human progress.

Understanding the Different Types of AI

The AI we use today for specialist tasks is called 'narrow AI', otherwise known as 'weak AI'. We call this type of artificial intelligence narrow or weak AI because it specializes in very specific domains.

The kind of AI that could truly think for itself and apply knowledge across multiple domains, similar to the way humans think, doesn't actually exist yet. That's currently a hypothetical stage of AI development that we refer to as Artificial General Intelligence (AGI) or 'strong AI'.

Here are some examples of what AGI could potentially do in the future:

- A personal assistant that does much more than schedule meetings or set reminders by also providing emotional support, managing finances, planning vacations, and even learning new skills on the fly.
- A universal problem solver, capable of solving complex scientific, medical, or philosophical problems without prior domain-specific programming.
- Adaptive robotics allowing robots to seamlessly transition from assembling cars to cooking meals or caring for older people with-

out reprogramming.

As this book is all about helping you integrate existing AI technologies into your life, we'll leave general AI in the realm of hypothetical possibilities and keep things simple by focusing only on the practical applications of narrow AI.

Narrow AI: The Specialist

Narrow AI systems are designed to perform a specific task or a limited set of functions with high efficiency. These systems are task-oriented and excel in environments where the objectives are well defined. While they can outperform humans in specific specialized tasks, they lack the ability to transfer their knowledge or adapt beyond their programmed functions.

Narrow AI is the dominant form of AI today, powering everything from recommendation algorithms to autonomous vehicles. Even though it's also called 'weak AI', it still packs a very powerful punch; processing vast amounts of data, detecting patterns, and making decisions more quickly and accurately than humans within its specific domain.

We can classify Narrow AI as Traditional AI or Generative AI depending on its purpose and the nature of its output. Here's how we do that:

Traditional AI: The Problem-Solver

Sometimes referred to as analytical AI, traditional AI is designed to analyze data, recognize patterns, make decisions, or provide recommendations based on structured rules and algorithms. These systems are typically task-specific, meaning they are trained for a single function and excel at solving repetitive, well-defined problems.

Many traditional AI systems use rule-based programming or machine learning models that rely on labeled data. They can process vast amounts of information, detect patterns, and apply predefined logic to make decisions with consistent and deterministic outcomes.

Examples of traditional AI:

- Medical diagnostic tools used to analyze symptoms and suggest possible illnesses
- Product and content suggestions based on past user behavior on platforms such as Amazon and Netflix
- Spotting suspicious transactions based on historical fraud patterns for banks and financial institutions
- Speech recognition systems such as Dragon NaturallySpeaking that convert spoken words into text

Generative AI: The Creator

Generative AI takes a more dynamic approach than traditional AI. As well as analyzing data and making predictions, generative AI can create entirely new content, including text, images, music, code, and even human-like speech.

Generative AI leverages deep learning techniques, particularly neural networks, to learn from vast datasets and generate outputs that resemble human creativity.

Unlike traditional AI, which follows a fixed decision-making framework, generative AI can produce unique, varied results each time it's prompted. It learns the patterns, structures, and nuances of human-generated content and synthesizes new material based on those insights. This type of creative AI continuously learns, adapts, and improves its outputs over time, making it incredibly versatile. But that's where ethical concerns about things like misinformation, copyright, and bias come into play.

Examples of generative AI:

- Text generation to write essays, generate code, and hold human-like conversations
- Image creation based on text descriptions
- Music composition of original songs in different styles
- Code writing to help developers by predicting and generating lines of code

This book focuses on generative AI because it's the most transformative advancement in the field, redefining how we create, solve problems, and automate tasks with unprecedented speed and flexibility.

While I'll occasionally reference traditional AI to provide context or highlight key differences, we're focused on where generative AI really shines, how to use it effectively, and why it has unmatched potential to reshape how we work, think, and innovate.

Test Your Understanding: Types of AI

Here's a list of popular AI tools you might have already encountered. Don't worry if you aren't familiar with them all, as we'll explore each of them in detail later in the book. In fact, this is a chance to start getting familiar with new AI tools right now!

For each one, decide whether it falls under Traditional AI (T) or Generative AI (G). Here's how you can tell the difference. If the tool primarily analyzes data to make decisions or perform tasks, it uses traditional AI. If it can create new content such as text, images, or music then it uses generative AI.

Try it yourself by writing 'Traditional AI' or 'Generative AI' next to each AI tool in the right-hand column. Then check your answers in the Answers Key below.

Table 1 Match the AI Tool to Its Type

	Traditional AI (T) or **Generative AI (G)**?
Chat GPT	
Gemini	
Google Translate	
Alexa	
Siri	
Midjourney	
Spotify's Music Recommendations	

- Is there any tool that surprised you in terms of their classification?
- How does knowing the difference between traditional and generative AI change how you view these tools?

Answers key:

- **ChatGPT → Generative AI (G)** *Generates human-like text based on user prompts.*
- **Gemini → Generative AI (G)** *Google's advanced AI model is capable of generating text, images, and more.*
- **Google Translate → Traditional AI (T)** *Translates text between languages using statistical models and neural machine translation.*
- **Alexa → Traditional AI (T)** *The voice assistant that performs tasks based on predefined functions and data analysis.*

- **Siri → Traditional AI (T)** *Apple's voice assistant responds to commands using traditional algorithms with some AI enhancements.*
- **Midjourney → Generative AI (G)** *Creates images from text prompts, showcasing AI-driven creativity.*
- **Spotify's Music Recommendations → Traditional AI (T)** *Analyzes listening habits to recommend songs based on algorithms and data patterns.*

How AI Wrote Itself into the History Books

The story of AI is just as exciting as the technology itself. While the idea of intelligent machines might seem like a modern concept, they have been part of human imagination for centuries, appearing in myths, stories, and early science fiction.

It was in the mid-20th century that AI began to take shape as a real scientific field, and in 1950, British mathematician Alan Turing posed a fundamental question: Can machines think?

He introduced what is now called the Turing Test – a method to evaluate whether a machine's responses are indistinguishable from those of a human. The test was a crucial early step in defining machine intelligence. A few years later, in 1956, researchers at the Dartmouth Conference – an annual event that explores the potential of artificial intelligence (AI) in business and society – formally coined the term 'artificial intelligence', marking the onset of AI as a dedicated field of study.

Over the next few decades, AI research went through cycles of breakthroughs and setbacks. Early AI programs from the 1960s to the early 1970s led to the creation of 'expert systems' – computer programs designed to mimic human decision-making in specific fields such as medical diagnosis – but progress slowed around 1974 as the new systems failed to meet high expectations. Interest in AI waned and much of the funding for AI research dried up as a result.

Following the 'golden years' of AI development in the 1950s, the period of reduced enthusiasm and investment from 1974 and well into the 1980s became known as the first AI winter.

There was a brief period of renewed interest in the late 1980s, but a second AI winter set in as research stagnated due to limited computing power and unrealistic ambitions.

Then, in the 1990s and early 2000s, the AI landscape changed dramatically with the rise of machine learning (ML); a type of AI that allows computers to recognize patterns and improve their performance over time by learning from data.

Unlike traditional programming, where humans write specific rules, machine learning enables AI to 'train' itself using large datasets. The real breakthrough came in 2012 with deep learning (a subfield of machine learning), which uses 'neural networks'; computer models inspired by the way the human brain processes information.

That year, a contender at the annual ImageNet software competition – a challenge in which AI models are tested on their ability to recognize objects in images – demonstrated the unprecedented prowess of deep learning architectures by achieving the lowest error score ever. The contender, AlexNet, won by a wide margin after processing well over a million images. This win for AlexNet effectively ended the cycle of AI winters, prompting revitalized research and development in AI with renewed enthusiasm for its newfound potential.

With these new breakthroughs, AI development progressed rapidly from 2018 to 2025, especially with the rise of large language models (LLMs) such as GPT-3 and GPT-4, which could generate human-like text, answer complex questions, and assist with tasks such as writing and coding.

The emergence of multimodal AI models was another major development as they became able to process and generate multiple types of data, such as text, images, and audio. An example of this enhanced capability is DALL-E, an AI system capable of generating images from text descriptions, showcasing how AI can be used for creativity and design.

As AI became more integrated into everyday life – powering personal assistants, creative tools, and even business decisions – global discussions intensified about ethics and regulation concerning the use of AI. As a result, the European Union introduced the EU AI Act in 2023. It was one of the first major legislative efforts to establish guidelines for responsible AI use, focusing on transparency, fairness, and safety.

Today, AI is still evolving at an unprecedented pace; shaping industries, creativity, and the way we interact with technology. Some call this period an AI renaissance, as we are witnessing a historic turning point, where AI has become an essential part of modern life.

Machine Learning and Neural Networks Made Simple

Keep in mind that machine learning is not a synonym for AI, but a crucial component of it, which enables machines to improve their performance without being explicitly programmed. In short, AI is the goal, and machine learning is a key method to achieve it.

When we think of machine learning, we should imagine a computer system that learns from experience, much like a child absorbing information from the world. Machine learning involves feeding data into algorithms that identify patterns and make decisions based on those patterns. This process mimics how humans learn from past experiences, allowing machines to recognize images, translate languages, and even predict future outcomes with remarkable accuracy.

The power of machine learning lies in its ability to process large volumes of data and extract meaningful insights, which can be applied across various fields, ranging from healthcare to finance.

Data is the lifeblood of machine learning. Without data, algorithms would have nothing to learn from. Machine learning collects, processes, and analyzes data to train models that can make predictions or decisions. This process is akin to teaching a child by providing examples and feedback, allowing them to learn from their mistakes and improve over time.

There are two primary approaches to machine learning: supervised learning and unsupervised learning.

In supervised learning, the model is trained on labeled data, meaning it learns from examples tagged with the correct answer, akin to a teacher guiding a student by providing the right solutions.

Unsupervised learning, on the other hand, involves training models on unlabeled data, allowing them to discover patterns and relationships without explicit guidance. This approach is similar to a child exploring their environment and making sense of it by themselves.

Neural networks inspired by the structure and function of the human brain are the backbone of many machine learning systems. These networks are made of interconnected nodes, also called 'neurons', to process and transmit information. Each neuron receives the input, processes it, and transfers the output to the next layer of neurons. This layered structure allows neural networks to learn complex patterns and make sense of intricate data.

Just as our brains process sensory information to recognize faces or understand speech, neural networks can identify objects in images, translate languages, and even generate realistic human-like text.

Machine learning and neural networks have become indispensable tools in real-world scenarios. Here are a few of them:

- Social media platforms use image recognition to automatically tag photos and identify relevant content for users.
- Chatbots leverage natural language processing to understand and respond to customer inquiries, providing efficient and personalized support.
- E-commerce companies employ predictive analytics to recommend products based on past purchases and browsing behavior, enhancing the shopping experience.

All these applications demonstrate the versatility and impact of machine learning and neural networks on our daily lives, transforming how we interact with technology and each other.

Algorithms are at the heart of machine learning and neural networks, driving their functionality. An algorithm is simply a set of instructions or rules to guide a process. In the context of AI, algorithms process data and learn from it to make predictions or decisions.

Consider the algorithms behind Google's search engine. While the search engine relies on machine learning to analyze vast amounts of indexed web data, it primarily focuses on retrieving and ranking links based on keyword relevance, page authority, and user behavior.

Advanced AI-powered search tools such as Perplexity.ai also use machine learning, but they do so with a different goal in mind. As well as finding and ranking pages, they also leverage natural language processing and generative AI to understand the context of your query to generate direct, conversational answers, often synthesizing information from several sources.

This shift illustrates how AI can evolve from simply retrieving information to actively interpreting and presenting it.

Try It Yourself: Google Vs Perplexity.ai

Let's do a quick experiment to demonstrate the difference between using these two types of machine learning. Think of a question such as *"What are the pros and cons of remote work?"*.

Start by putting the question to Google. You'll probably see a mix of links to articles and a quick summary at the top. That's Google's AI-generated snippet, which is designed to give you a fast answer. To get the whole picture, you might still need to click a few links and read through different sources to find your answers.

Now type the same question into Perplexity.ai and see a very noticeable difference in the results. Instead of just pointing you to links, Perplexity gives you a direct, detailed response, often summarizing key points from multiple sources all in one place. In this case, it literally creates a comprehensive list with headers for pros and cons.

- Which felt quicker or clearer?
- Did your interaction with Perplexity feel more like having a con-

versation than Google just guiding you to explore on your own?

This simple exercise shows us how different search engines use AI in different ways – Google helps you find information while Perplexity generates direct answers to your questions.

Build Your AI Vocabulary

Talking about AI is understandably uncomfortable when you're not familiar with the topic. Imagine attending a gathering where everyone speaks a language you're just beginning to learn. The words sound familiar, yet their meanings elude you, creating a barrier to fully engaging in conversation. That's how many beginners feel when they first encounter the world of AI.

If you come across any words you don't know, look in the **Comprehensive AI Glossary** among the additional resources linked at the beginning of this book.

With each new term you master, the world of AI becomes less daunting as the intricacies and possibilities are revealed.

Test Your Understanding: Are You Familiar with the AI Jargon?

Try this quick exercise to assess your familiarity with key AI terms you've encountered so far, along with a few new ones. Match each AI term from 1 to 8 with the correct definition or application (a - h).

1. **Algorithm**

2. **Machine Learning**

3. **Neural Networks**
4. **Natural Language Processing**
5. **Deep Learning**
6. **Reinforcement Learning**
7. **Predictive Analytics**
8. **Computer Vision**

a. A branch of AI that deals with understanding and generating human language.
b. The process by which computers improve automatically through experience.
c. Statistical algorithms used to predict future outcomes based on historical data.
d. A type of model particularly adept at processing pixel data for image recognition tasks.
e. The step-by-step procedures for solving problems or performing tasks.
f. A learning method where systems learn optimal behaviors through rewards and feedback.
g. Systems inspired by the human brain comprising interconnected nodes.
h. The application of AI to interpret visual data, such as medical images.

Now reflect on your answers and revisit any terms that remain unclear in the **Comprehensive AI Glossary**. This interactive approach solidifies your knowledge and demonstrates how AI terms interconnect, contributing to a broader understanding of the field.

Continue to familiarize yourself with the glossary to build a strong foundational knowledge of the terms and equip yourself to explore AI's potential with enthusiasm and insight.

How AI is Already Part of Your Daily Life

Now that you understand what AI is at its core, we can recognize it more easily in our daily lives. Let's explore some of these instances together, and you'll see everything begin to resonate.

Imagine waking up to the gentle sound of your smartphone's alarm, the time set by your virtual assistant based on your schedule, the weather, and traffic conditions.

As you reach for your phone to check the day's agenda, you're interacting with AI without even realizing it. This seamless integration of AI into our daily routines is both convenient and transformative.

Voice assistants such as Siri or Google Assistant in smartphones have become invaluable companions, helping us manage tasks, answer questions, and even control smart home devices. These assistants rely on AI to understand and respond to our voice commands, making our interactions with technology more intuitive and efficient.

Navigation apps are another example of the subtle yet powerful presence AI has in our lives. When you're commuting or exploring a new city, these apps use AI to analyze real-time traffic data, predict delays, and suggest optimal routes.

We save more time and experience less stress as a result, allowing us to focus on the journey itself rather than the logistics. The ability of AI to quickly process vast amounts of data accurately means that we continually benefit from its insights, often without realizing the complexity behind the scenes.

Beyond our personal devices, the influence of AI extends to consumer products that enhance our daily experiences. Streaming services, for instance, use AI algorithms to analyze your viewing habits and preferences, recommending content tailored to your tastes.

This personalization enriches our entertainment experience, introduces us to new genres and shows that we might not have otherwise discovered.

When linked up with smart homes, AI-enabled devices can automate tasks such as adjusting thermostats, managing lighting, and securing entryways. While these innovations enhance our quality of life with increased convenience, they also improve energy efficiency and security.

In commerce, all kinds of businesses are now leveraging AI to drive efficiency and innovation in their respective industries. In healthcare, AI systems help doctors diagnose diseases by analyzing medical images to detect anomalies that might be missed by the human eye. This capability improves accuracy and speeds up the diagnostic process, ensuring timely treatment for patients.

In finance, AI plays a crucial role in fraud detection, analyzing transaction patterns to identify suspicious activities and protect consumers from financial losses. The agriculture sector also benefits from AI's capabilities, with AI-powered drones and sensors monitoring crop health and optimizing resource use, ultimately boosting yields and sustainability.

The ubiquity of AI technologies across various domains highlights their profound impact on productivity and decision-making. Productivity tools, for example, leverage AI to automate repetitive tasks, freeing up time for their users to pursue more creative and strategic endeavors.

Social media platforms utilize AI algorithms to curate content, ensuring that users see posts most relevant to their interests, while also managing the vast amounts of data generated by billions of interactions.

In entertainment, AI powers recommendation engines and content creation, enhancing the way we consume and engage with media.

As we navigate this AI-driven landscape, we must recognize the mix of opportunities and challenges accompanying these advancements. While AI enhances efficiency and convenience, it also raises questions about data privacy, ethical considerations, and the potential for bias in decision-making processes. Being mindful of these implications ensures that we can fully embrace the benefits of AI while addressing its limitations and risks.

It's clear by now that AI plays many roles in our daily lives, from simplifying tasks to offering personalized experiences and driving industry innovation.

When we understand how AI operates behind the scenes, we become more informed and empowered users, capable of leveraging its capabilities to enhance our personal and professional endeavors. As we continue to engage with AI, let us remain curious, open to learning, and committed to using this technology responsibly, ensuring that its impact aligns with our values and aspirations.

Moment of Reflection: Your Daily AI interaction

As you delve deeper into the world of AI, take a moment to reflect on how AI affects your day-to-day activities. Consider the tools you use, from smartphones to online platforms, and identify which ones incorporate AI.

- How does AI enhance your experience?

- What limitations do you notice?

Reflect on your initial perceptions of AI and how they might evolve as you explore its capabilities and applications.

Reflecting this way gives grounding to your understanding and prepares you to embrace AI with an informed and open mindset.

In the next chapter (Chapter 2), we'll dive into using some of the most popular generative AI tools. At that point, you'll get the chance to try out a free version of any tool you like and see how it matches up with your reflections. It's a fun way to check whether AI is involved in any of the activities you're already doing. You can even ask the tool itself what it thinks about AI's limitations and how it might evolve in the future.

2

GET STARTED WITH AI TOOLS

Navigating the rapidly evolving landscape of diverse AI tools coming online can be daunting at first, but this smart new tech is easier to use than ever before.

Almost everyone has heard of the conversational AI tool ChatGPT, which was launched in late 2022 by the artificial intelligence research organization OpenAI. Within a week of its launch, the very user-friendly chatbot had more than a million users, growing exponentially to well over 180 million users worldwide today.

ChatGPT's popularity comes down to it being free to use and highly versatile without any programming skills required, so it's easily accessible to almost anyone with a computer or mobile device. It uses a large language model (LLM) to converse with users and help perform a wide variety of tasks, ranging from drafting emails to brainstorming creative ideas, making it a valuable asset in enhancing personal productivity.

ChatGPT is commonly used as a gentle introduction to the world of AI because its intuitive design is super easy to interact with, but the power under its hood has had an undeniably huge impact on the way we use AI tools to help us with all kinds of tasks.

ChatGPT and Beyond

If you're exploring AI for the first time, ChatGPT offers a straightforward way to start learning and creating content. As a form of conversational AI, it engages you in natural, human-like discussions, processing your input to generate responses that feel intuitive and contextually relevant.

ChatGPT can help speed up almost any writing task, such as drafting a report or preparing a presentation by quickly structuring your ideas, suggesting relevant information, and refining your language; making communication clearer and more effective. Its ability to generate content based on your prompts allows you to explore different perspectives, making it a valuable partner in the creative process. Whether you're brainstorming ideas, drafting an email, or fine-tuning your writing, ChatGPT is a highly versatile tool for personal and professional applications.

You'll explore the many ways ChatGPT can enhance various areas of your daily life in Part II, alongside image generators, data synthesis tools, and music creation platforms. For now, though, we'll focus specifically on conversational AI tools.

Conversational AI is one of the most accessible and widely-used forms of generative AI, making it an ideal entry point for beginners. It plays an integral role in everyday life; powering virtual assistants, customer support chatbots, and AI-driven writing tools. Understanding how conversational AI works gives you a solid foundation for engaging with more advanced AI systems in the future.

Several other AI tools beyond ChatGPT offer distinct capabilities catering to different needs. Google's Gemini, for example, is designed to enhance workplace productivity by optimizing workflows through predictive analytics. To this end, Gemini has additional features to improve team collaboration and efficiency, such as generating checklists of suggested next steps at the end of meetings, assigning due dates, and identifying primary stakeholders for each task.

Gemini also supports more than 40 languages, and has the ability to recall past conversations, providing users with contextually relevant responses without the need to revisit previous discussions.

The Chatbot Claude, developed by Anthropic, excels in natural language processing tasks and long-form text generation. It's designed to handle large volumes of contextual information, allowing users to upload text files for analysis. It also emphasizes safety and ethical considerations in its responses, often refusing to engage with prompts it deems unsafe.

Grok is a generative artificial intelligence chatbot developed by xAI, an artificial intelligence company founded by Elon Musk. It's marketed as an advanced chatbot available to premium subscribers of X (formerly Twitter). It's also based on the large language model with the aim of integrating analytical reasoning with conversational capabilities, providing real-time insights and enhanced reasoning capabilities. Newer versions of Grok have introduced a 'Big Brain' mode, boosting its ability to handle complex problem-solving tasks with greater computational power.

Another emerging player in the AI space is DeepSeek, a conversational generative AI model developed by a Chinese startup founded by Liang Wenfeng. DeepSeek has rapidly gained popularity since its launch in December 2023. Unlike many mainstream models, DeepSeek is particularly effective at complex, multi-step reasoning while maintaining strong multilingual comprehension. Its efficiency lies in delivering high performance, even with lower computational resources, making it an increasingly attractive option for anyone seeking a good balance of capability and efficiency.

I always recommend that beginners starting out on their AI journey first explore free AI tools. Free versions are a low-risk way to experiment and gain hands-on experience without the pressure of financial commitment. They offer an accessible and user-friendly entry point, allowing you to test different capabilities and familiarize yourself with AI's potential. However, it's important to recognize the limitations that often come with free models, such as feature restrictions, data privacy concerns, and the presence of ads or upsell prompts. Despite these constraints, these free tools serve as an invaluable introduction to AI and provide a solid foundation for more advanced exploration.

When you're ready to take your AI interactions to the next level, experiment with platforms such as Galaxy.ai and the paid version of ChatGPT, both of which offer expanded functionalities in a single package. These comprehensive suites integrate a variety of AI tools designed to boost productivity and streamline tasks, making them an appealing choice for users wanting to maximize the benefits of AI in their personal and professional lives. In Galaxy.ai, you can also switch between different AI conversational models (ChatGPT, Claude, DeepSeek, etc.) within the same chat to best fit your next question.

By starting with free tools and gradually transitioning to more advanced options, you can soon build confidence in using AI and develop a deeper understanding of how it can enhance different aspects of your daily life. The key is to approach it with curiosity, experiment with different models, and find the tools that best meet your specific needs and goals.

How to Evaluate AI Tools Before You Invest

When you're ready to invest in more advanced AI tools, first evaluate your needs and compare them to the features different models offer. Having a clear framework to evaluate your needs helps you make the most informed and appropriate choice.

Your framework should focus on four main criteria: ease of use, compatibility with existing systems, customization options and quality of output. These considerations form the bedrock of selecting an AI tool to complement your workflow rather than complicating it:

Ease of Use

A tool with an intuitive user interface makes your interaction seamless, reducing the learning curve, which is particularly important for beginners feeling overwhelmed by complex layouts or unclear instructions.

Compatibility

Compatibility ensures the tool integrates smoothly with your current devices and software, minimizing disruptions.

Customization

Customization options allow you to tailor the tool to your specific needs, enhancing its usefulness.

Quality of Output

A tool with high-quality output consistently provides accurate, reliable, and engaging content, helping you achieve your goals effectively. This means fewer worries about incorrect information, biased responses, or superficial analysis. With high-quality output, you can confidently rely on the tool for creative, analytical, or professional tasks.

The table below is an example of how you can create a framework to evaluate the strengths and weaknesses of the AI tools you plan to experiment with.

Table 2 Overview of Most Popular Generative AI Tools

	Free Version	Paid Version	Strengths	Weaknesses	Best Used For
ChatGPT	Yes - Basic text responses	Yes - Faster responses, multimodal tools included	- Best multimodal AI - Strong creativity - Broad tool integration - Supports text, images, and code in paid version	- Primarily text-based - Prone to generating incorrect or biased information	Creative writing, productivity, multimodal AI
Gemini	Yes - Text and basic multimodal support	Yes - Advanced AI Model, better app connections, more powerful features	- Multimodal processing even in free version (text, images, audio, video) - Integrated with Google Workspace - Strong ethical considerations (integrated within Google's regulated ecosystem)	- High computational requirements - Less customizable	Task automation, search-enhanced AI workflows
Claude	Yes - Text-based AI with context memory	Yes - Faster responses, more detailed answers, higher usage limits	- Emphasis on safety and transparency (predefined ethical principles) - Fast response times - Good at intuitive data understanding	- Occasional capacity constraints - Less depth in complex analyses	Long-form text analysis, ethical AI
Grok	Yes - Basic chatbot on X (formerly Twitter)	Yes - Enhanced reasoning with Big Brain mode, higher limits	- Real-time data access from X - Humorous and unfiltered responses - Photorealistic image generation	- Primarily limited to X platform - Potential for biased or unverified information	Social media insights, real-time data
DeepSeek	Yes - Multilingual AI with deep reasoning	Yes - API access for developers and commercial use	- Strong at handling multiple languages - Good for logical problem-solving and complex reasoning - Open-source and resource-efficient	- Privacy concerns due to data storage in China - Avoids sensitive political topics	Multilingual communication, deep analytical AI

Note: The information provided is based on available data as of March 2025 and may be subject to change.

To effectively align AI tool features with your specific needs, clearly identify any non-negotiable features that you must have to achieve your goals and include them in your framework. If data security is a priority, give preference to AI tools offering robust encryption and privacy controls.

To get the best value for money, also aim for a balance of cost versus functionality by prioritizing tools that directly service your needs and address the challenges you face.

Some tools may offer extensive features but they usually come with a hefty price tag. On the other hand, a tool with fewer features might be all you need, and at a fraction of the cost. Getting this balance right is key to enhancing your productivity with AI tools in a cost-effective manner.

How to Identify Trustworthy AI Tools

You may still feel overwhelmed by the plethora of AI tools becoming increasingly available – with each new tool touted as the new frontier in AI for a particular domain – so how do you ensure that a new tool is trustworthy?

Start by examining the developer's credentials and the company's reputation. Well-established companies usually provide more reliable and secure tools than newer competitors because they have a legacy of trust to maintain.

Look for companies with a history of innovation and customer satisfaction. Check whether they have partnerships with well-known tech firms or endorsements from industry experts. These signs can indicate a commitment to quality and reliability, helping you make an informed decision.

User reviews and testimonials are another valuable resource. These first-hand accounts offer insights into the experiences of other users. Pay attention to patterns in feedback.

It's common to see one or two negative reviews from users who might have experienced issues for obscure reasons beyond the developers' control, so don't let those reviews bother you too much. Instead, assess whether users are consistently praising or criticizing the same features, which gives you a clearer picture of the tool's strengths and potential shortcomings. Remember, no tool is flawless, but consistent complaints about functionality or customer service should raise a red flag.

Transparency in data usage policies is also crucial. Trustworthy tools provide clear information about how they collect, store, and use your data. They should have easily accessible privacy policies and adhere to recognized standards such as General Data Protection Regulation (GDPR) compliance. This ensures that your data is handled responsibly and ethically.

In your quest to find dependable AI tools, be hyper vigilant about potential scams and overhyped products. Any unrealistic claims about the capabilities of a new AI tool that promises overnight results can often be too good to be true.

Genuine AI tools are transparent about their limitations and the effort required to achieve desired outcomes. Be wary of those promoted with flashy marketing but little substance. Also consider the level of support offered. Tools lacking customer support or documentation could leave you stranded if issues arise. Reliable tools usually have robust support systems, including tutorials, FAQs, and dedicated customer service teams ready to assist you round the clock.

Data privacy is a growing concern in the digital age so ensuring the AI tools you use comply with privacy standards is paramount. Tools that prioritize secure data handling practices often use encryption and other safeguards to protect your personal information. These safety features protect you against unauthorized access and go a long way to reinforcing trust in the tool.

When you're identifying trustworthy tools, keep in mind that you should be looking for a balance of functionality and security with reliable support.

Using this approach mitigates risks and empowers you to leverage AI's potential without compromising your data's integrity. Armed with these fundamental insights, you'll be well equipped to make informed decisions for a safe and rewarding venture into AI.

Try It Yourself: Getting Started with ChatGPT

For the purposes of this book, we'll be using the free version of ChatGPT as the base conversational tool for our exercises and examples, because it is easily accessible, user-friendly, and designed to help anyone. Even so, feel free to use any other conversational AI tool if you prefer.

To get started, try asking the following question as an example, and wait for ChatGPT's response:

"What's a creative birthday gift idea for someone who loves books?"

- Did ChatGPT's response demonstrate a clear understanding of your question?
- How could you apply similar queries to your daily life?

This is just the beginning!

How to Use AI Tools for Everyday Tasks

AI tools are no longer confined to high-tech environments. They're already integral to our daily routines, helping us improve productivity, manage personal health and development, and enhance creativity.

Incorporating AI into everyday tasks makes life a lot easier to manage more efficiently by significantly streamlining activities. Although it can be daunting at first, using AI soon becomes second nature with a few strategic steps.

Enhancing productivity with AI is more than just automating tasks – it's about freeing up mental space for more important activities.

AI excels at handling repetitive chores, enabling you to focus on strategic initiatives, creative pursuits, and personal growth. You can seamlessly integrate AI into almost every facet of your life to organize your schedule, manage your finances, support your health goals, and be a launch pad for creative endeavors. In fact AI tools have opened brand new avenues for fostering unlimited creative expression and innovation.

In Part II, you'll explore how to apply the concepts we've discussed here in real-world scenarios. Each subsequent chapter guides you through specific domains in which AI can make a tangible difference by equipping you with practical tools to harness its full potential in your daily life.

Moment of Reflection: Explore Your Best AI Solutions

Take a moment to reflect on which areas AI could benefit you the most. Think about your current routines, challenges, and tasks you'd like to streamline or enhance.

This will give you a feel for actively engaging with AI tools to evaluate their practicality and make informed decisions about integrating them into your life.

1. Identify a task or challenge in your daily life that you believe could be improved with AI.
2. Open ChatGPT and enter the flexible prompt below to explore

possibilities:

"Suggest the most effective AI solution for [insert your task/challenge here]. *Provide advice on the feasibility of achieving this with AI, specify if it can be done using ChatGPT, recommend any additional AI tools that could be useful, and outline a simple decision-making framework to help me choose the best option."*

See how you can use a multi faceted prompt to summarize what you want the AI tool to do for you.

By experimenting with different tasks, you'll gain a clearer understanding of how AI can be tailored to meet your specific needs.

PART II: PRACTICAL APPLICATIONS OF AI IN DAILY LIFE

3

BOOST PRODUCTIVITY AND EFFICIENCY WITH AI

Whether you're juggling multiple responsibilities at work, managing household chores, or planning your next vacation, AI can assist you with all these activities and more.

Let's dive into the transformative ways AI can help you work more efficiently, stay organized, and ultimately achieve more with less effort.

Smarter Task Management

AI tools are excellent for optimizing task management, letting you focus on what truly matters so you can start your day with all your tasks seamlessly organized and prioritized with hardly any effort on your part.

The online workflow platform Trello, for example, enhances organization by analyzing workflow patterns and suggesting optimizations that save time and reduce stress. It categorizes tasks based on urgency and importance, ensuring you tackle the most crucial ones first.

Similarly, AI assistants such as Google Assistant refine scheduling by learning from your habits. With voice commands you can set reminders, schedule meetings, and check travel times, all tailored to your routine. Using these kinds of tools as personal assistants frees you from planning so you can focus on strategic decisions.

AI's impact on productivity goes far beyond organization; it actively improves how we approach tasks. By automating routine activities, AI saves time that you can redirect to creative and more complex projects.

AI algorithms can automatically sort and prioritize emails in your overwhelming inbox so you see only the most relevant messages. And, AI-driven to-do lists such as Microsoft To Do offer personalized task recommendations based on your behavior and deadlines. With these intelligent systems adapting to your workflow, you can maintain a high level of focus and efficiency throughout the day.

The tools just mentioned are based on traditional AI. You can further enhance your productivity by benefiting from ChatGPT's generative capabilities as it works alongside traditional AI tools. By summarizing tasks, prioritizing deadlines, and offering tailored productivity tips, ChatGPT is a highly versatile assistant. It can break down projects into steps, track progress, and suggest efficient ways to tackle tasks. Simply interacting with ChatGPT by itself is a great help for streamlining workload and clarifying objectives.

Think of ChatGPT as a smart coordinator as you work with other tools. For example, instead of manually adding tasks to Trello, you can describe your project to ChatGPT and it'll suggest task lists already formatted for easily entering in Trello.

If you use Google Assistant for scheduling, ChatGPT can summarize meeting notes and create a clear list of follow-up tasks. This way, ChatGPT boosts existing tools, reducing manual effort in task management.

Table 3 AI Tools for Task Management

	ChatGPT	Trello	Google Assistant	Microsoft To Do
Type of AI	Generative AI	Traditional AI	Traditional AI	Traditional AI
Free Version	Yes - Basic chatbot for task ideas	Yes - Task boards and lists	Yes - Reminders, lists, basic voice AI	Yes - Task lists, reminders, sync.
Paid Version	Yes - Advanced features	Yes - Automation, integrations, advanced views	No (Accessed through Google devices)	No
Strengths	Highly adaptable, generates creative task ideas, suggests workflow improvements, supports complex prompts	Strong visual task organization, easy collaboration, integrates well with team tools	Efficient voice commands, real-time reminders, hands-free task management, seamless integration with Google services	Seamless integration with Microsoft apps, intuitive task lists, good cross-device sync
Weaknesses	Lacks built-in project structure, no automatic organization of tasks over time, manual effort required	Limited AI automation, relies on manual inputs, not ideal for dynamic tasks	Basic task features, lacks depth for complex projects, dependent on voice accuracy	Minimal AI capabilities, limited automation, not optimized for large team projects
Best Used For	Brainstorming, planning, summarizing, generating task lists, strategic thinking	Project tracking, team tasks	Quick reminders, managing appointments, hands-free tasks	Personal task lists, reminders

Note: The information provided is based on available data as of March 2025 and may be subject to change.

Integrating AI into your daily workflow does require some thoughtful planning, but the benefits are well worth the initial effort. Begin by assessing which areas of your life can benefit most from automation. It could be for managing appointments, keeping track of deadlines, or breaking a big project into a more manageable list of tasks.

Once you've identified those areas, choose AI tools that align with those needs. Start small, leveraging ChatGPT as a support tool. To begin with, you could use AI to automate responses to frequent email queries, or to set recurring reminders for weekly meetings. Then, expand the scope of AI's role in your productivity system as you become more comfortable using it.

Customize each tool's settings as you go, to match your specific needs, ensuring they work seamlessly within your existing workflow. Over time, you'll find that as well as simplifying task management, AI also enhances your ability to focus, innovate, and achieve your goals.

Try It Yourself: Organize Your Day

Try the simple exercise below to experience how ChatGPT can help you organize your day in just a few short steps.

Open ChatGPT and type the following prompt:

"Help me organize my daily tasks. I need to manage work projects, personal errands, and self-care activities."

Don't overthink your prompts. Just describe your day the same way you'd tell a friend. That's the beauty of ChatGPT. It understands natural language, so there's no special format required.

Wait for ChatGPT to respond.

- Does its suggestion resonate with you?
- Could you refine your prompt any further based on your specific needs?

ChatGPT will adapt to your needs when you tell it to, offering personalized suggestions that help you focus on what matters most.

Simplified Text Management and Organization

Using AI as a virtual assistant is a game-changer for managing your digital life, saving many hours of work each week. In fact, regular AI assistant users say they can save up to four hours a day by using AI-powered text management and organization tools, according to the *2024 Global Workforce of the Future Survey* by one of the world's largest human resources service providers, Adecco Group.

With a rudimentary AI assistant at your beck and call with text management and organizing capabilities, you can turn chaos into order with minimal effort by automating routine text-related tasks.

Think back to the last time your email inbox was a chaotic mess of unread messages, spam, and important emails buried under promotions. Sound familiar?

The built-in sorting features in Gmail or Outlook already use traditional AI to tidy up your inbox by telling it to categorize emails and sort them into relevant folders. Automated email categorization works by analyzing messages and classifying them according to your preferences, ensuring priority emails stand out while promotional content is discreetly set aside.

These kinds of AI-driven document summarization tools can save you lots of reading time by quickly extracting key insights from reports and giving you concise summaries, empowering you to make quicker, better informed decisions.

Beyond sorting emails and summarizing documents, AI-powered search and retrieval systems have redefined the way we access information, especially when generative AI capabilities are at work. Today's advanced algorithms can sift through vast volumes of data to give us tailored results.

AI makes quick work of scouring databases or past chat conversations to glean the information you need without endless scrolling. It's a hassle-free way to access precisely what you need in an instant – boosting productivity and easing the burden of managing large volumes of text.

ChatGPT is a good starting point for getting used to working with text management tools. Beginners can easily harness its intuitive, prompt-based interface without any coding knowledge at all.

With contextual understanding and coherent responses, ChatGPT acts as a reliable digital assistant to help draft emails based on unstructured notes or ideas, generate content outlines, and brainstorm reports.

AI-powered note-taking tools are a boon for entrepreneurs or anyone wanting to streamline project management. They do much more than just taking notes.

The Notion app, for example, has an optional paid AI add-on available for its free and paid software that is a handy tool for enhancing productivity by summarizing content, generating ideas, and improving note clarity. It also integrates smoothly with ChatGPT so you can draft ideas in ChatGPT, then refine them in Notion AI for structured project management as well.

Grammarly is a writing assistant that does a lot more than checking your grammar. It helps you write clearly and concisely using a blend of traditional and generative AI to refine tone, clarity, and style to ensure your writing is polished and professional.

Otter.ai excels at real-time transcription. It uses traditional AI to transcribe meetings, identify different speakers, and generate searchable notes. Once your meeting is transcribed, you can feed notes into ChatGPT to create summaries, draft follow-ups, or generate action items.

QuillBot is a generative AI tool that simplifies and tightens text, making reports clearer and more concise. You can draft content in ChatGPT and then refine it with QuillBot to improve readability.

We can see from these examples that you can build a powerful ecosystem for text management by combining ChatGPT with specialized AI tools –

enhancing productivity, improving organization, and reducing the mental load of handling large amounts of information.

Table 4 AI Tools for Text Management & Organization

	ChatGPT	Notion AI	QuillBot	Grammarly	Otter.ai
Type of AI	Generative AI	Generative AI	Generative AI	Traditional AI + Generative AI	Traditional AI
Free Version	Yes - Basic text generation, limited queries	NO (Paid add-on to Notion)	Yes - Basic paraphrasing, limited modes	Yes - Grammar/ spelling checks, basic suggestions, limited generative AI features	Yes - Limited transcriptions, basic features
Paid Version	Yes - Advanced features, longer responses	Yes - AI automation, advanced organization tools	Yes - Advanced paraphrasing, summarization tools	Yes - Tone, clarity, style enhancements	Yes - More transcription hours, advanced tools
Strengths	Generates diverse content quickly, adapts to various writing styles	AI organizes, summarizes notes, enhances project workflows efficiently	AI excels at paraphrasing, summarizing text concisely and effectively	AI improves grammar, tone, clarity, ensures professional text quality	AI-driven transcription captures speech accurately, identifies speakers
Weaknesses	AI lacks deep content organization, limited contextual memory	AI depends on user input, struggles with nuanced content creation	AI struggles with context-heavy content, relies on existing drafts	AI can't create original content, focuses on corrective functions	AI limited to transcription tasks, accuracy drops with poor audio
Best Used For	Drafting content, idea generation, summaries	Organizing notes, documents, and managing projects	Simplifying content, rephrasing, summarizing	Polishing text, improving clarity and style	Transcribing meetings, creating searchable notes

Note: The information provided is based on available data as of March 2025 and may be subject to change.

The boom in AI text management tools has had a profoundly positive impact on our practical lives. An academic researcher using AI to streamline data collection and analysis now has a lot more time on their hands for critical thinking and hypothesis development. Likewise, a content manager who relies on AI to organize and tag vast amounts of digital content enjoys much greater efficiency in their workflow.

Integrating AI systems into existing workflows is really quite easy. Once you've customized the settings, you'll be all set to let AI do much of the legwork while you focus on more strategic activities. Begin by identifying areas where AI can provide the most value, such as automating repetitive tasks or enhancing document management. Set up collaborative platforms that let you integrate other AI tools so you and your team can work together efficiently. Customize AI settings to match your organizational needs, tailoring features such as tagging, categorization, and summarization to align with your goals.

Try It Yourself: Draft an Email with ChatGPT

Try this exercise to see just how effective using ChatGPT can be in saving time and effort when writing a professional email by using a simple prompt.

Let's say you've just finished a meeting about a project you are working on and want to debrief your team, client, or supervisor. Write down a quick, unstructured list of points discussed. Try entering the following prompt template in ChatGPT and wait for the outcome:

"Organize these notes into a clear, structured email update to [team/client/supervisor], highlighting key achievements, current status, and next steps. Keep the tone [friendly/formal/concise]."

Based on the template above, your prompt might actually look something like this:

"Organize these notes into a clear, structured email update to my supervisor, highlighting key achievements, current status, and next steps. Keep the tone concise and professional.

Notes:

Finished initial design mockups, client approved them yesterday Development team started coding the main features Encountered minor delays due to technical issues, but resolved quickly Currently on track to meet the original deadline Next week: internal testing phase begins, prepare test cases.

Need supervisor to confirm availability for review meeting next Thursday"

- Does the email created by ChatGPT sound clear, concise, and professional and were the key points organized effectively?
- What changes, if any, would improve the output?

Personal Finance Strategies Made Easy

If managing your personal or business finances is overwhelming, you can easily use AI-powered tools to simplify the process and do a lot of the leg work for you. They'll keep track of bills and transactions for you, and provide personalized budgets with real-time expense tracking to boot, so you always stay on top of your finances.

The personal financial management app Mint (Intuit Mint) uses traditional AI to categorize transactions and alert you to unusual spending, making it easier to monitor finances without combing through statements.

Similarly, the automated investment service Wealthfront provides AI-driven financial advice by analyzing data to suggest investment strategies tailored to your goals.

These are just two of the many AI-driven tools designed specifically to streamline the financial management process, giving you more time to focus on financial well-being.

The benefits of managing your finances with AI go way beyond basic budgeting though. With built-in predictive analytics, AI-powered financial tools can also help you make better long-term plans and smarter financial decisions by forecasting future spending trends based on past behavior. These tools can also categorize transactions and analyze spending patterns to give you deep insights into where your money goes, helping you identify areas for savings.

Using these tools is like having a personal financial advisor available day and night to give you instant insights. When you use a data-driven approach to your finances, you become empowered to make smarter financial choices and stay on track to comfortably achieve your savings goals.

ChatGPT supports personal finance management in versatile ways. It can generate personalized financial advice, draft budget plans, and create financial checklists based on your unique needs.

You can ask ChatGPT to summarize financial documents, suggest cost-cutting measures, or help set financial goals. If you provide ChatGPT with details such as income and expenses, it can draft a budget for you, suggest spending limits, and recommend adjustments. For smaller datasets, you can directly paste data and tables into ChatGPT for analysis. With the paid version of ChatGPT (ChatGPT Plus), you can even upload spreadsheet files directly. However, for larger or more complex datasets – and as you become more confident using AI – it's best to integrate

ChatGPT with spreadsheet tools such as Google Sheets or Excel. This integration allows you to automate data analysis, summarize financial data, and generate dynamic budget reports directly within your spreadsheet. To connect ChatGPT with spreadsheets, you can use APIs (Application Programming Interfaces) or third-party integrations. Both methods enable apps to communicate and exchange information: APIs require custom coding and offer greater flexibility, while third-party integrations such as Zapier and Make are ready-made, no-code solutions, which are ideal for beginners.

This might sound a bit complex but it basically means that you can use ChatGPT to analyze the data exported by the financial tools such as Mint or Wealthfront. For example, Mint tracks expenses and then exports the data as a spreadsheet. You then use ChatGPT to interpret the data within those spreadsheets to identify trends and suggest improvements with actionable budgeting steps.

Similarly, after Wealthfront offers investment strategies, ChatGPT can break them down into manageable tasks or clarify the financial jargon for you.

So, by using ChatGPT with traditional AI tools, you can create a dynamic financial system that blends data-driven insights with real-time support – a synergy that makes finance management highly efficient and adapts to your changing needs.

If you want an all-in-one solution without the extra hassle of using ChatGPT, there are dedicated generative AI tools on the market such as Cleo and FinChat, each of which already integrates personalized, conversational insights directly within budgeting and investing workflows.

Cleo, which is primarily available and widely used in the United States, is very user friendly and offers AI-driven financial coaching plus budgeting and savings suggestions.

FinChat simplifies investment research with real-time insights, stock analysis, and financial report summaries.

Table 5 AI Tools for Personal Finance Management

	ChatGPT	Cleo	FinChat	Mint	Wealthfront
Type of AI	Generative AI	Generative AI	Generative AI	Traditional AI	Traditional AI
Free Version	Yes - Basic chat, financial advice	Yes - Budgeting tips, expense tracking	Yes - Basic investment insights, stock analysis	Yes - Tracks expenses, categorizes spending	No - Some free tools available for AI-driven financial planning (not investments)
Paid Version	Yes - Direct spreadsheet uploads for data analysis	Yes - AI coaching, premium insights	Yes - Advanced analytics, premium financial reports	Yes - Ad-free, advanced features	Yes - Automated investment management and portfolio optimization
Strengths	Flexible, personalized advice, budget planning, scenario analysis	Engaging chatbot, smart budgeting tips, spending insights	Investment insights, simplification of financial data, real-time analysis	Automated categorization, real-time alerts, intuitive dashboard	Sophisticated investment algorithms, tax-loss harvesting, automation
Weaknesses	No direct data linking requires manual input, lacks automation	Surface-level analysis, less detailed financial projections	Focused on investments, lacks budgeting tools, limited to financial data	Limited for complex financial needs, ads in the free version	Focuses solely on investments, lacks budgeting features
Best Used For	Custom financial insights, goal planning	Engaging budgeting tips, spending habits	Investment research, stock analysis, financial reporting	Expense tracking, budget monitoring	Automated investing, portfolio management

Note: The information provided is based on available data as of March 2025 and may be subject to change.

Financial assistants are great for managing family finances, too. They make taking care of personal finances easier than ever. It's like having a professional bookkeeping service on hand for little to no cost.

Families can successfully meet their savings goals using insights from AI budgeting tools that analyze spending patterns and identify areas for adjustment to optimize their budget based on discretionary income.

Individuals facing more severe financial struggles can turn to AI tools to help them work towards financial stability with debt reduction strategies.

As AI technology evolves, its role in personal finance will only grow, offering increasingly sophisticated solutions tailored to individual needs.

Try It Yourself: Design Your Budget

Try using ChatGPT to create a personalized budget tailored to your financial goals by using the following prompt:

"Help me create a personalized budget. My monthly income is [insert amount], and my fixed expenses include rent ([amount]$), utilities ([amount]$), groceries ([amount]$), and transportation ([amount]$). I'd like to save for [goal, e.g., vacation, emergency fund, debt repayment]."

See how ChatGPT responded and consider these questions:

- How did ChatGPT's suggestions align with your current budgeting habits?
- What insights did you gain about your spending or savings goals?
- How would you continue using ChatGPT to track or refine your budget?

AI-Powered Home Organization

With AI-powered household management, you can enjoy the futuristic convenience of having a home that practically manages itself, even while you're away. What was once a vision of the future is now a modern-day reality with household management systems giving you reminders and even preparing grocery lists.

Tools such as Google Home and Amazon Alexa have transformed how we interact with our living spaces. They simplify daily routines and make our homes smarter and more efficient by allowing us to effortlessly manage tasks with simple voice commands.

Google Home can handle reminders, calendar events, and even play your favorite playlist while you prepare breakfast, while Alexa can seamlessly adapt to your lifestyle by integrating with smart home devices to control lighting, security and more.

Can we take household management even further with generative AI tools such as ChatGPT?

Yes. Unlike traditional AI, which relies on pre-programmed responses, ChatGPT goes beyond basic commands to offer dynamic, context-aware support by generating personalized suggestions and detailed to-do lists.

Setting up and customizing AI assistants is actually very easy, even for beginners. With a few clicks you can configure basic settings to match your family's schedule and set reminders for key tasks such as taking out the trash or watering the plants to ensure nothing gets overlooked. You can also sync calendar events so everyone stays informed about appointments and activities.

Now imagine what you can do by integrating ChatGPT with AI tools such as Google Calendar or smart home hubs. By leveraging APIs or third-party integrations, you could easily ask ChatGPT to draft a weekly cleaning schedule and automatically sync it with your calendar to automatically give you timely reminders without manual input.

Other emerging generative AI tools such as Milo and Ohai are revolutionizing household management by reducing the mental load on busy families.

Milo acts as an AI co-pilot for parents by effortlessly organizing family information. Send Milo text messages, photos of permission slips, or school sign-ups and it processes the data to predict next steps. It can also add reminders to your calendar or send alerts for upcoming events.

Ohai's AI assistant is also geared towards efficiently managing family schedules, especially childcare needs. It scans emails to create calendar events, resolves scheduling conflicts, delegates tasks, and even books appointments by phone. Its proactive recommendations make it a powerful household management tool.

Such personalization makes AI assistants an integral part of our households, seamlessly adapting to anticipate our needs. By blending generative AI such as ChatGPT, Milo, and Ohai with traditional AI platforms, you create an intelligent home environment that enhances your daily life with nothing more than a few voice commands.

When AI-powered devices are connected to smart home appliances, you can schedule cleaning tasks, send reminders for laundry, or even adjust the thermostat based on your habits. Automating these tasks so you don't forget to turn off the heating or the dishwasher really helps reduce energy consumption and bring you cost savings. When you no longer have to spend so much time on all those mundane tasks, you have ample free time to focus on more meaningful activities.

Table 6 AI Tools for Household Management

	ChatGPT	Milo	Ohai	Alexa	Google Home
Type of AI	Generative AI	Generative AI	Generative AI	Traditional AI	Traditional AI
Free Version	Yes - Basic chat features	No	No	Yes - Voice commands, basic automation	Yes - Voice assistant, simple controls
Paid Version	Yes - Advanced plugins, faster peak-time access	Yes	Yes	Yes - Smart home integrations, premium skills	Yes - Advanced routines, smart device control
Strengths	Flexible, context-aware responses, task automation, adapts to diverse needs	Predictive task management, family-focused AI, integrates with calendars, reminders	Automates complex scheduling, proactive support, handles tasks without prompts	Quick voice commands, strong smart device integration, hands-free control	Seamless Google ecosystem, calendar syncing, efficient for smart home management
Weaknesses	Needs manual integration for calendars, tasks; limited real-time automation	Limited outside family tasks, learning curve for new users, less broad scope	Less flexible for non-family tasks, relies heavily on proactive data input	Limited conversational depth, basic responses, dependent on device ecosystem	Dependency on Google services, less custom AI, limited outside Google ecosystem
Best Used For	Personalized planning, flexible household tasks	Family schedule organization, reminders	Complex family scheduling, proactive assistance	Voice-controlled home automation	Managing smart devices, syncing with Google apps

Note: The information provided is based on available data as of March 2025 and may be subject to change.

The benefits of using AI for home management go beyond convenience. While their efficiency helps you save time and money on routine chores, they are also adept at keeping you safe.

With an AI-driven surveillance system integrated with your home security solution, you have peace of mind that your home is being constantly monitored by advanced cameras and sensors which will automatically alert you of any suspicious activity.

Try It Yourself: Design Your Ideal Household Routine

Experience firsthand how ChatGPT can be your personal household assistant by asking it to help create a customized daily routine that fits your lifestyle.

Try asking ChatGPT something like this:

"I need help creating a personalized daily routine to manage my household tasks more efficiently. I usually wake up at [insert your wake-up time], and my key priorities are [list your tasks: cleaning, cooking, work, family time, etc.]. I prefer to [mention your preferences: "get chores done early," "have free evenings," etc.]. Can you design a simple, realistic schedule for me?"

The more details you give, the more personalized your routine will be. Don't worry if it's not perfect. You can tweak it later.

- What surprised you about ChatGPT's suggestions?
- Can you think of other areas in your household where ChatGPT could help?

Effortless Travel Planning

With the help of AI, you can make meticulous travel plans to ensure every detail is organized, leaving you free to actually enjoy the adventure.

The trip planner TripIt has revolutionized how we plan travel itineraries by using traditional AI to organize flight schedules, hotel bookings, and various activities into a cohesive plan.

With TripIt, you can effortlessly consolidate all your travel information in one place and view your itinerary at a glance. It automatically updates any changes, ensuring your travel plans remain current and hassle-free.

Another travel app called Hopper uses traditional AI to offer predictive flight booking. It does this by analyzing millions of data points to recommend the best times to book flights for optimal savings. By using AI to predict price trends, Hopper helps you plan the best time to book a deal in the future rather than the ones immediately available, making travel more affordable and accessible in the long run.

To enjoy an even more personalized approach, use tools such as ChatGPT and GuideGeek to harness the power of generative AI and get suggested travel itineraries tailored to your interests.

By engaging with ChatGPT, you can explore various destinations and get customized recommendations based on your preferences. Whether you're interested in exploring historical landmarks, indulging in culinary delights, or seeking outdoor adventures, ChatGPT will offer suggestions that suit your travel tastes.

GuideGeek is specially designed to be a savvy travel assistant that really understands your needs. It leverages generative AI and is built directly on ChatGPT technology to provide personalized travel advice based on real-time data, helping you plan itineraries with recommendations that resonate with your unique interests.

The AI in these travel planners give you a highly personalized experience by grabbing information about the places you plan to visit so it can familiarize you with things like dining options in the surrounding area that suit your taste, including any dietary needs, and give you the lowdown on customer reviews. Whether you're after fine dining or a casual meal with locals, you'll get recommendations based on your preferences.

Table 7 AI Tools for Travel Planning

	ChatGPT	GuideGeek	Hopper	TripIt
Type of AI	Generative AI	Generative AI	Traditional AI	Traditional AI
Free Version	Yes - Basic travel suggestions, itinerary ideas	Yes - Personalized travel advice via messaging	Yes - Price tracking, booking suggestions	Yes - Basic itinerary organization, updates
Paid Version	Yes - Advanced features, faster responses	No	No	Yes - Pro features like real-time alerts
Strengths	Highly customizable, broad knowledge base, versatile across travel topics	Real-time personalized advice, user-friendly, great for quick recommendations	Accurate price predictions, data-driven insights, strong booking optimization	Automatic itinerary updates, easy consolidation, seamless trip organization
Weaknesses	Lacks real-time travel data integration, limited for live updates	Limited to messaging platforms, less flexible for complex planning	Focus on prices, less itinerary flexibility, not for detailed planning	Less personalized recommendations, rigid structure, minimal customization
Best Used For	Personalized itineraries based on preferences	On-the-go travel tips, quick recommendations	Finding best booking times, saving money	Organizing and tracking travel plans easily

Note: The information provided is based on available data as of March 2025 and may be subject to change.

Using these AI-powered guides means you'll get to explore more than the average Joe. The curated recommendations will deepen your travel experience by connecting you with new places and cultures. You'll even get recommendations for hidden gems and lesser-known attractions off the typical tourist path. ChatGPT can help you get prepared right down to the finest detail with a personalized packing list based on your destination plus activity and trip length information.

As an example of the kind of flexibility AI gives you when planning trips, you'll get very different suggestions for a weekend cultural getaway compared to an adventure holiday. For a cultural getaway, AI might recommend a renowned museum, a historic walking tour, and a traditional dinner at a local eatery. But if you're looking for adventure, the AI might come up with an itinerary that includes a theme park, a nature hike, and an interactive science museum.

For solo and family adventures alike, integrating AI into your travel planning gives you so many more options to explore the world, and helps you find ways to do it cost effectively with optimized routes and local insights – making for more memorable and meaningful trips. If it's just the two of you on a romantic getaway, AI can bring those travel dreams to life, too.

Try It Yourself: Design Your Perfect 3-Day Travel Itinerary

Now try using ChatGPT to create a customized 3-day itinerary based on your interests and travel style by giving it a prompt like this one:

"Plan a 3-day itinerary for [City You Love] tailored to a [Type of Traveler You Are – e.g., foodie, history enthusiast, nature lover, adventure seeker, or art aficionado]. Include recommendations for must-see attractions, local dining spots, hidden gems, and tips for maximizing my time."

You can modify the prompt by adding details about your budget, preferred pace (relaxed or packed schedule), or specific activities you enjoy. The more information you give ChatGPT, the more refined your itinerary becomes to make the trip uniquely yours.

- Were the recommendations relevant and appealing to you?
- Would you rely on AI like ChatGPT for future travel planning?

4

AI FOR PERSONAL DEVELOPMENT AND SELF IMPROVEMENT

Setting and achieving personal development goals is hugely challenging, especially as learning new life skills is usually a solo journey requiring a great deal of discipline to overcome hurdles that can appear insurmountable at first.

Whether you're learning a new language or trying to educate yourself to climb higher up the career ladder, having an AI assistant by your side makes that journey a lot easier to plan and strategize for success, because you aren't doing it alone anymore.

Assigning AI the role of your personal development coach helps you break down those overwhelming goals into manageable steps in a highly personalized plan of daily disciplines to keep you on track with reminders of your daily goals and suggestions on how best to achieve them.

This is the evolving role of AI in personal development as a dynamic partner in your growth journey. From guiding your learning process to breaking through language barriers, AI empowers your goal-setting efforts with tailored insights and tools that adapt to your unique aspirations.

Over the next few pages, we'll explore how AI is transforming personal development through personalized learning paths, advanced language support, and effective goal-setting strategies. Each subchapter will demonstrate how you can harness AI to enhance personal growth, making self-improvement more accessible, efficient, and aligned with your personal vision.

The Future of Learning Through AI

AI has made online learning accessible to everyone with the ability to create a virtual classroom where each student receives personalized attention with lessons tailored to their pace and learning style.

AI's ability to serve up interactive content is a major advantage in keeping students engaged with multimedia elements, gamified quizzes, and instant feedback on their own progress – all of which keep students highly motivated.

Several online learning platforms for young and adult learners have sprung up in the past decade by leveraging the personalization power of AI to engineer highly adaptive teaching assistants.

AI teaching assistants such as Khanmigo, the generative AI used by online learning hub Khan Academy, make this customized learning approach possible by adapting content to individual needs.

When you sign up for a course with the Khan Academy, Khanmigo creates personalized learning paths for students by assessing their individual skills and abilities, then adjusts the difficulty based on the student's performance. This tailored approach ensures learners stay engaged without feeling overwhelmed or bored.

Other learning platforms for adults such as Coursera and Udemy also use AI to recommend courses based on individual participant's interests and career goals, personalizing the learning journey for them. In addition, generative AI in Coursera makes it possible for instructors to easily develop comprehensive course materials and quizzes for students – and students themselves get automated feedback to help them refine their work by highlighting strengths and areas for improvement.

AI-generated simulations can also create dynamic learning environments, allowing students to engage with realistic scenarios and apply theoretical knowledge in practical settings.

The learning app Socratic primarily uses traditional AI and machine learning to interpret student questions, retrieve relevant information, and provide clear explanations, enhancing its responses by guiding students to useful educational resources.

Educators themselves can more easily assess student progress with much greater efficiency with help from AI analytics, allowing them to refine teaching strategies and address individual learning gaps. This data-driven approach saves a lot of time and frustration for educators and students alike, drastically improving the quality of the education offered by enabling teachers to focus on inspiring and guiding individual students toward success.

Again, ChatGPT serves as a versatile learning companion here by helping students simplify complex topics and generate study summaries. It can even create flashcards and simulate quizzes based on the course material. ChatGPT's linguistic abilities also make it particularly effective for language learning, which we'll explore later.

Educators can also make good use of ChatGPT to design lesson plans, generate discussion prompts, and provide instant writing feedback. Chat-

GPT's adaptability in this respect makes it useful for students of all ages as well as educators in any field of academic and self-directed learning.

As you can see from these examples, AI is helping education move forward in many diverse ways, supporting a diverse variety of learners ranging from homeschool students to lifelong learners crafting a dynamic career path. By providing personalized guidance and access to a gold mine of resources, AI empowers individuals to take control of their education with a much higher degree of confidence than in conventional classroom settings.

Table 8 AI Tools for Educational Support

	ChatGPT	Khanmigo	Coursera	Socratic
Type of AI	Generative AI	Generative AI	Traditional AI + Generative AI	Traditional AI
Free Version	Yes - Basic Q&A and text generation	No (Pilot free access for teachers)	Yes - Course previews, limited access	Yes - Homework help and explanations
Paid Version	Yes - Advanced features, faster responses	Yes - Subscription for students and parents	Yes - Full courses, certificates, projects, generative AI features	No
Strengths	Versatile, adaptive, great for brainstorming, Q&A, and content generation	Personalized learning paths, interactive tutoring, leveraging Khan Academy extensive resources, strong in math/science	Structured learning, course recommendations, professional development, certifications	Quick answers, visual explanations, simple interface for homework help
Weaknesses	Lacks deep subject expertise, may generate inaccurate info	Limited depth in non-core subjects, limited access in some regions	Less interactive, passive learning, key features behind paywall	Surface-level help, lacks depth for complex topics
Best Used For	Study aid, content generation, Q&A	Personal tutoring, math/science guidance	Structured learning, professional development	Quick homework help, basic concept review

Note: The information provided is based on available data as of March 2025 and may be subject to change.

The positive impact AI has on education is evident in many success stories from students and educators.

The *Digital Education Council Global AI Student Survey 2024*, for example, reported that out of thousands of students questioned in 16 countries, 86 percent of them are already using AI to support their studies.

Students struggling to grasp traditional learning methods are increasingly turning to AI tutoring for support with personalized lessons and real-time feedback, discovering a new found love of learning in the process and seeing dramatic improvements in their grades.

Educators, too, have embraced AI to address diverse classroom needs, frequently using analytics to better understand student performance and adapt their teaching methods. A 2025 report by Adobe on *Creativity with AI in Education* revealed that 85 percent of about 3,000 educators surveyed in the US and UK believe that generative AI has the ability to increase students' creativity and creative thinking skills.

These examples highlight the potential of AI to further transform education by offering innovative and practical solutions. As AI continues to evolve, its role in shaping the future of learning will only grow, making education more accessible and effective for all.

Try It Yourself: Boost Your Learning on a Specific Subject

Discover how ChatGPT can act as your personalized learning assistant by helping you understand complex topics, create study aids, and simulate exam questions. Pick a subject you're currently studying or interested in and ask it the following prompts:

- *"Explain [your topic] to me like I'm a beginner."*
- *"Summarize the key points of [your topic] in bullet points."*
- *"Create 5 multiple-choice questions about [your topic] with correct answers."*

Review the answers and consider:

- Did the explanation make the topic clearer?
- How accurate and detailed were the quiz questions?

Break Down Language Barriers

Conversing with locals in foreign lands is a lot easier these days with AI breaking down language barriers in translation apps as well as powering language learning courses.

You might have used Google Translate before, which uses traditional AI to help you understand text or common phrases in other languages. The language learning app Duolingo also uses traditional AI but goes a step further to enhance language acquisition by incorporating adaptive learning algorithms to tailor lessons that match your progress and keep students engaged as tasks become more challenging – catering well to beginners and advanced learners alike.

The language learning app Rosetta Stone also uses traditional AI to help you learn hundreds of different languages through immersive techniques. What sets it apart from other language apps is its ability to listen to you and simulate practicing with a native speaker, while giving you pronunciation feedback and real-time corrections, so it's a great confidence booster in this respect.

Generative AI tools such as DeepL and ChatGPT take language learning further by providing dynamic, real-time conversational practice. You can role-play with ChatGPT as a travel companion, business colleague, or local shopkeeper to broaden your vocabulary while improving sentence structure and fluency. ChatGPT also offers instant translations, grammar explanations, and customized exercises tailored to your learning goals.

DeepL is a powerful AI language tool and writing companion that uses generative AI to enhance language learning with advanced translation and writing support. It helps refine sentence structure, expand vocabulary, and adjust tone for clarity and style across several different languages.

Table 9 AI for Language Education

	ChatGPT	DeepL Write	Duolingo	Rosetta Stone
Type of AI	Generative AI	Generative AI	Traditional AI	Traditional AI
Free Version	Yes - Basic conversations, language queries	Yes - Basic writing improvements, clarity	Yes - Basic lessons, adaptive practice	No
Paid Version	Yes - Advanced features, longer context handling	Yes - Advanced tone/style suggestions	Yes - Offline access, advanced lessons	Yes - Full courses, personalized feedback
Strengths	Dynamic, real-time conversations, grammar explanations	Enhances clarity, style adaptation, grammar suggestions, multilingual support	Gamified, adaptive learning, engaging activities, personalized progress tracking	Immersive learning, real-time pronunciation feedback, structured lessons
Weaknesses	Lacks structured curriculum, inconsistent accuracy in complex topics	Limited for conversation, bias towards formal tone, less interactive	Limited speaking practice, repetitive exercises, lacks deep cultural context	Less engaging for casual learners, slower progress without motivation
Best Used For	Conversational practice, language exploration, grammar support	Writing improvement, style refinement, multilingual editing	Vocabulary building, grammar exercises, beginner language basics	Pronunciation, structured language courses, formal language training

Note: The information provided is based on available data as of March 2025 and may be subject to change.

These easily accessible tools are examples of how AI can be a catalyst for democratizing language learning, offering opportunities to anyone with a digital device and a desire to learn and expand their linguistic horizons.

Students learning a second or third language are also reaping the benefits of AI-assisted study sessions giving them tailored lessons and real-time feedback to quickly improve grades and comprehension.

Try It Yourself: Feel the Difference Between ChatGPT and Google Translate

To see for yourself how ChatGPT's generative AI differs from traditional AI tools such as Google Translate, try this simple exercise:

Come up with a sentence in English that includes figurative language, idioms, or cultural context – something similar to this: *"I can't believe she let the cat out of the bag".*

Enter the sentence in Google Translate and translate it into a different language. Any language will do. Then translate the foreign language back into English and note whether Google Translate handles the ambiguity correctly.

Now try translating the same sentence in ChatGPT with a command like this: *"Translate into [target language]: I can't believe she let the cat out of the bag".*

Then get ChatGPT to translate the original translation back into English.

- Was there any difference in the back and forth translations?
- Which version feels closer to the original intention?

Empower Goal Setting with AI

Setting and achieving personal goals is a cornerstone of personal development but maintaining consistency is always a struggle. With AI, you now have access to sophisticated tools that help you define your objectives and keep you motivated with continuous support and progress tracking.

ChatGPT can step in to help out here as an interactive goal-setting assistant. All you have to do is articulate your goals in a conversational way with ChatGPT and it'll use established frameworks such as SMART (Specific, Measurable, Achievable, Relevant, Time-bound) to clarify your objectives. By answering a series of guided questions, you can refine vague goals into clear, actionable statements.

As mentioned before, ChatGPT's generative AI can deconstruct big ambitions into manageable tasks, creating step-by-step plans. On top of that, ChatGPT offers words of encouragement, gives you reminders, and offers up reflective prompts to keep you focused on the end goal. With instant access to your dialogue history, ChatGPT can also reference past interactions to monitor ongoing achievements and suggest adjustments whenever needed.

AI-powered coaching platforms Replika and Rocky.ai both use generative AI to offer personalized coaching and mentoring experiences with enhanced goal setting and habit tracking functions.

Replika engages users in human-like conversations, offering a supportive and interactive environment to discuss and reflect on personal goals. It encourages self-reflection and provides motivational support, helping users explore and set personal development objectives.

If getting fitter is your goal, the coaching app Rocky.ai is an expert at helping you build a fitness routine and keep you pumped with daily motivational check-ins and habit-building prompts tailored to your personal goals. Rocky.ai focuses on personal development, leadership growth, and forming positive habits through conversational AI to help you learn new skills and stay motivated.

Traditional AI tools are more suited to support habit formation strategies. Streaks, for example, is a to-do list app that relies on traditional AI to help you form good habits by identifying patterns in habit completion, plus it gives you insights to identify areas where you're struggling.

The self-care coaching app Fabulous is another habit-building app you can use to improve your morning routine that uses traditional AI to keep you in check. It can help you develop healthy routines through personalized coaching, science-based habit formation techniques, and give you motivational prompts that'll inspire you to build lasting habits with personalized habit suggestions and daily coaching tips.

Table 10 AI Tools for Goal Setting

	ChatGPT	Replika	Rocky.ai	Streaks	Fabulous
Type of AI	Generative AI	Generative AI	Generative AI	Traditional AI	Traditional AI
Free Version	Yes - Basic conversations and goal prompts	Yes - Basic chat, limited topics, and personalization	Yes - Basic coaching prompts	No	Yes - Habit tracking with limited coaching
Paid Version	Yes - Advanced features & custom responses	Yes - Advanced customization, voice calls, augmented reality features	Yes - Tailored coaching & growth plans	Yes - Advanced habit analytics & reminders	Yes - Personalized routines & coaching programs
Strengths	Highly adaptable, broad conversational support, flexible for diverse topics	Engaging, personalized interactions to motivation and emotional support,	Motivational coaching for habit formation, promotes consistency and self-discipline	Simple, effective visual habit tracking with strong focus on daily consistency	Science-backed routines with personalized tips, great for structured habit growth
Weaknesses	Lacks structured goal tracking features, requires manual effort for progress tracking	Limited structured goal-tracking frameworks and detailed analytics for goal achievement	Basic coaching compared to human coaches, limited depth in complex goal areas	Limited to habit tracking, not coaching, lacks personalized development insights	Less dynamic AI compared to generative AI, limited adaptability in responses
Best Used For	Personal goal reflection and idea generation	Exploring goals with an emotional support, self-reflection	Daily motivation & habit coaching	Tracking and maintaining consistency with daily habits	Holistic approach to habit formation and personal growth

Note: The information provided is based on available data as of March 2025 and may be subject to change.

As you can see, AI's ability to adapt to an individual's evolving vision is what makes it a reliable ally in the struggle to achieve long-term goals, especially the way you can combine goal setting with habit tracking to keep pushing you forwards with a dynamic feedback loop.

Using generative AI tools really helps you visualize your long-term aspirations with the ability to generate mind maps or narrative frameworks for you. But the kind of feedback you get from both generative and traditional AI is ideal for keeping short-term goals aligned with your overarching personal development objectives.

To gain useful insight into which goal-achieving strategies are best for you, all you have to do is feed the AI with data about your goals and the progress you've made. It'll then analyze the data and highlight trends that'll help you make adjustments.

Whichever app or platform you chose, incorporating AI into goal setting and habit tracking empowers you to pursue personal development with clarity, consistency, and adaptability.

Try It Yourself: Create a Personalized Development Plan

Before opting for a dedicated coaching app, dip your toes in the water by trying out ChatGPT to help you set meaningful goals, reflect on progress, and gain motivational support.

Use the prompt below to ask ChatGPT for help:

"I'd like you to act as my personal coach. Help me set a goal to improve [insert your focus area]. Ask me questions to clarify my goal and create an action plan."

ChatGPT will ask you questions to narrow down your needs by guiding you to reflect deeply on them so you can uncover new insights to shape your action plan collaboratively.

- How did ChatGPT's questions help you think differently about your goal?

- What was the most helpful advice or insight you received?
- How could you continue using ChatGPT for personal growth in the future?

5

AI FOR HEALTHIER LIVING AND WELL-BEING

Looking after our health and wellness is an individual journey. There isn't a standard one-size-fits-all approach, which is why AI is an ideal wellness guru to have by your side.

Similar to the personal development apps we discussed earlier, health and wellness apps can use AI to analyze data, track progress, and adapt recommendations to improve your overall well-being.

Whether you want to enhance your workouts, simplify healthy eating or build a more mindful routine, AI can offer tailored support to fit your lifestyle. In this chapter, you'll explore how AI can support your wellness journey by helping you make informed decisions, stay consistent, and ultimately lead a healthier, more balanced life.

Power Up with AI-Generated Personalized Fitness Plans

Reaching your personal fitness goals is a lot easier when you have an AI fitness trainer in your pocket that knows your routine and can adapt to your body and goals.

The resistance training app Fitbod optimizes and adapts your fitness program by analyzing your fitness data to create tailored workout plans. The app can track your performance through wearable monitoring devices such as Apple watches, and offer insights into strengths and areas for growth by continuously evolving your fitness journey.

As well as keeping you motivated and challenged with AI-generated fitness plans, the tailored programs they provide based on your limitations won't overwhelm you with impossible goals. They'll also make informed adjustments to minimize the risk of injury by suggesting safe alternatives in a proactive approach that keeps you focused on progress without worrying about overexertion or improper technique.

Fitter is another app using AI to revolutionize personal fitness. It leverages generative AI to design evolving workout programs based on goals, fitness level, and available equipment.

Fitness apps using traditional AI are good at analyzing data but those using generative AI are better able to continually adapt to your progress and create dynamic plans that change with your needs.

In this respect, ChatGPT's generative AI can take on the personal trainer role with enhanced personalized fitness planning. You can assign it to generate customized workouts, suggest modifications based on feedback, and keep you motivated just like a human coach would. On top of all that, ChatGPT can design comprehensive fitness schedules that include exercises, recovery strategies, nutrition tips, and even mental wellness support – making it a powerful tool for holistic health management.

These coaching apps can bring a wealth of benefits across the whole spectrum of health and wellness needs, from weight loss regimes to winning strategies for serious athletes.

Table 11 AI Tools for Fitness

	ChatGPT	Fitter AI	Fitbod
Type of AI	Generative AI	Generative AI	Traditional AI
Free Version	Yes - Basic Q&A, simple plans	Yes - Limited custom plans available	Yes - Basic workout suggestions
Paid Version	Yes - Advanced coaching, tailored programs	Yes - Full personalized programs, advanced tracking	Yes - Full personalization, progress tracking
Strengths	Flexible coaching, versatile advice, highly adaptive across fitness, recovery, and wellness needs	Dynamic personalized plans, adaptive over time with real-time adjustments based on progress	Strong data analysis, tracks progress well, optimized for strength training routines
Weaknesses	Lacks real-time physical feedback, not specialized in fitness-specific tracking or metrics	May lack detailed nutritional integration, limited non-fitness wellness support	Limited flexibility for unique workout needs, rigid structure for advanced athletes
Best Used For	Custom coaching, flexible fitness routines	Dynamic personalized workout programs	Tracking strength progress, structured plans

Note: The information provided is based on available data as of March 2025 and may be subject to change.

Individuals struggling with weight management have successfully reached their body goals using AI as a personal nutritionist to serve up dietary suggestions and meal plans. At the professional end of the spectrum, athletes and sports coaches for example have found that AI can enhance performance on a whole new level by analyzing individual athlete's performance. A 2024 report by Forbes, *How AI Is Revolutionizing Professional Sports*, revealed athletic improvements in speed, gait patterns, and endurance with the help of these apps.

Marathon runners have credited AI training apps with helping them improve their personal best times by using the tech to analyze past runs and get recommended pace adjustments as well as specific drills to boost their speed and endurance.

These kinds of enhancements in performance are success stories that are only possible with the insight AI can provide, right down to the finest details, offering the kind of guidance that was once only accessible through personal trainers.

Try It Yourself: Design Your Personalized Workout

To experience how generative AI can create a personalized fitness plan for you, try using the flexible prompt below to ask ChatGPT for a workout plan tailored to your needs. You can modify the details to fit your goals, current fitness level, and available equipment.

"Create a workout plan to help me improve [specific area of your body, e.g., core strength, upper body, legs, flexibility]. I currently [describe your fitness level, e.g., beginner, intermediate, advanced], and I have [mention any equipment you have or say 'no equipment']. My goals are [state your goals, e.g., build muscle, lose weight, improve endurance], and I prefer workouts that are [mention preferences like short, low-impact, or high-intensity]."

After filling in the details, your request might look something like this: *"Create a workout plan to help me improve my core strength. I am a beginner with no equipment. My goal is to build core stability, and I prefer low-impact exercises."*

Also try asking follow-up questions to adjust the routine if needed, just as you would with a personal trainer.

- Does the workout plan align with your goals and preferences?
- Are there any exercises you'd like to modify or replace?
- How well does ChatGPT adapt the plan if you request changes?

Create Customized Meal Plans

Meal planning for dietary needs is a juggling act that's especially challenging when you're catering to an entire family's diverse needs. Fortunately,

AI platforms have stepped in to simplify this process, offering tailored meal plans that cater to individual tastes and nutritional goals.

These dietary needs are where tools such as meal planning app Mealime and recipe discovery app Yummly really shine. They can cater to your specific dietary needs, whether they are from gluten-free options or high-protein diets, and craft a meal plan just for you.

Mealime uses traditional AI to suggest recipes to fit with your dietary preferences, taking into account your likes, dislikes, and any dietary restrictions you might have. The app filters recipes based on your criteria, ensuring you only see options that suit your palate and nutritional needs.

Aside from these dedicated meal-planning apps, ChatGPT itself can serve as a powerful tool for nutrition and meal customization. You can prompt ChatGPT to generate meal plans based on specific dietary goals such as weight loss, muscle gain, or just to achieve balanced eating habits. Unlike pre-programmed meal-planning apps, ChatGPT actually gives you greater flexibility in adjusting meals on the fly; offering suggestions for substitutions, portion adjustments, or budget-friendly ingredient swaps. Additionally, it can create personalized grocery lists based on your preferences and even generate creative recipes using only the ingredients you have on hand.

Other AI-driven tools are also expanding the possibilities of meal planning and nutrition tracking such as January AI, which is a generative AI-powered platform that can predict the impact of different foods on blood sugar levels, helping users make informed dietary choices. It can even analyze photos of meals and make an educated guess about the ingredients for you.

Similarly, Samsung Food – an AI-powered personalized food and recipe service – employs generative AI alongside computer vision (a type of traditional AI) to recognize over 40,000 food ingredients through a smartphone camera. With these functions the app generates recipe suggestions, personalized meal plans, and performs nutrition tracking tasks.

These are just a few of the advancements made with AI to reshape the way we approach food and its role in maintaining good health, making meal planning smarter, easier, and more tailored to individual needs.

Table 12 AI Tools for Meal Planning and Customization

	ChatGPT	January AI	Samsung Food	Mealime
Type of AI	Generative AI	Generative AI	Traditional AI + Generative AI	Traditional AI
Free Version	Yes - Basic meal ideas, general advice	Yes - Food impact analysis, glucose tracking	Yes - Identifies ingredients, suggests recipes	Yes - Recipe filtering, meal plan suggestions
Paid Version	Yes - Advanced AI prompts, deeper customization	Yes - More insights, deeper meal tracking	No	Yes - More personalized plans, grocery lists
Strengths	Highly flexible, customizable meal suggestions; adapts to dietary needs	Predicts food impact, health-focused AI insights; helps manage glucose levels	Recognizes ingredients, suggests recipes, adapts meals, integrates with smart appliances	Easy to navigate, structured meal plans, quick filtering for diet preferences
Weaknesses	No built-in grocery list integration; requires manual meal structuring	Requires health data; setup can be complex for first-time users	Limited personalization beyond ingredient-based suggestions; lacks deep nutrition tracking	Less dynamic AI; does not adjust in real-time for dietary needs
Best Used For	Personalized meal plans with full flexibility	Health-conscious meal planning & tracking	Ingredient recognition & quick meal ideas	Simple, structured meal planning

Note: The information provided is based on available data as of March 2025 and may be subject to change.

Creating a personalized meal plan with AI starts by inputting your personal data, including dietary goals – whether losing weight, building muscle, or just eating healthier is your aim. By setting nutritional targets such as daily calorie intake or macronutrient ratios, AI tailors meal suggestions to help you meet them.

Customization options let you specify food allergies or preferences, ensuring the AI avoids ingredients that don't fit your needs. This means your meal plan isn't generic, since it's designed specifically for you.

Time saving is a major advantage with AI meal planning. Bespoke diets need a lot more prep than microwaved TV dinners. Even deciding what to eat for a week means coming up with dozens of different recipes, and then you have to shop for it all too. AI can do all the planning for you by generating recipe ideas and shopping lists to get the groceries you need for those recipes. The AI also balances macronutrients, ensuring you get the right mix of proteins, fats, and carbohydrates to support energy levels and fitness goals.

If you're going vegetarian for the first time, you could try AI-generated meal plans for a beginner-friendly vegetarian week. AI might suggest hearty lentil stew or quinoa salad to ensure you still get essential nutrients. For fitness enthusiasts, AI could create a high-protein plan with meals like grilled chicken with vegetables or tofu stir-fry, supporting muscle growth and recovery.

These AI-powered meal planning abilities simplify decision-making and help you make well informed dietary choices. With AI as your culinary assistant, maintaining a balanced diet becomes an efficient, enjoyable experience without all that meal prepping stress.

Try It Yourself: Create a Personalized Recipe

Use ChatGPT to generate a recipe based on your dietary preferences and the ingredients you have on hand with a prompt like this:

"I follow a [dietary preference, e.g., vegan, keto, gluten-free]. I have these five ingredients: [list five ingredients that you have at home]. Can you suggest a recipe using only these ingredients? If any substitutions are needed, please suggest alternatives. Also, are there any limitations in making this meal fully compliant with my dietary preference, based on the ingredient provided?"

- Does the recipe fully align with your dietary preference?
- Did ChatGPT suggest useful substitutions?
- Were there any limitations in creating a balanced meal with just these ingredients?

Enhance Your Mindfulness Routine

Although distancing ourselves from tech and hectic schedules is often associated with improving mindfulness, we can't all just drop everything and disappear for a weekend retreat in the woods. On the other hand, AI has actually become a powerful tool for practicing mindfulness while keeping up busy routines. It can support relaxation and present-moment awareness in many ways, even for the busiest parents and professionals among us.

AI-powered apps make mindfulness more accessible and customizable, helping you integrate personalized practices into daily routines. Guided meditation, immersive soundscapes, and AI-generated exercises designed to foster calm and balance can all be part of your mindfulness program with these digital tools.

Some apps personalize meditation sessions based on preferences and progress, while others use generative AI to create custom prompts and reflections. You can go about your day with earphones immersing you in AI-generated sound environments to help you focus or relax and fall asleep to, making mindfulness an effortless part of daily life.

Several AI applications stand out in this space. Endel is a generative music mobile app that creates personalized sound environments in real time to match your activities and adapt based on things such as the time of the day, weather, and even your heart rate.

Vital is an AI-powered meditation app that calms you with audio-guided meditation experiences tailored to your individual preferences, and the app Youper, originally designed for emotional well-being, includes AI-driven meditation tools to support self-awareness and inner peace.

You can also use ChatGPT to enhance mindfulness practices by asking it to generate custom meditation scripts, give you mindfulness reminders and reflective journaling prompts. With a few well-crafted inputs, you can create personalized exercises, including grounding techniques, breathing exercises, and gratitude practices.

Table 13 AI Tools for Mindfulness

	ChatGPT	Endel	Vital	Youper
Type of AI	Generative AI	Generative AI	Generative AI	Traditional AI
Free Version	Yes - Text-based mindfulness prompts & journaling	No	No	Yes - AI mindfulness exercises & mood tracking
Paid Version	Yes - Advanced prompts & structured guidance	Yes - Personalized & adaptive soundscapes	Yes - Personalized meditation experiences	Yes - Deeper insights & expanded mindfulness tools
Strengths	Highly flexible, personalized mindfulness chat & journaling	Immersive AI-generated soundscapes for deep relaxation & focus	Dynamic AI-powered meditation tailored to user progress	AI-driven mindfulness support, mood tracking, structured exercises
Weaknesses	No audio guidance, lacks structured mindfulness flow	Not interactive, limited meditation guidance, only sound-based	Newer tool, less recognition & evolving AI personalization	Less interactive, does not generate personalized conversations
Best Used For	Custom mindfulness exercises & reflective journaling	Creating immersive soundscapes for relaxation and focus	Personalized guided meditation and mindfulness exercises	Mindfulness with structured mood tracking & insights

Note: The information provided is based on available data as of March 2025 and may be subject to change.

Starting on a path to mindfulness can be a bit of a minefield for beginners, especially if you're trying to integrate calming practices into a busy lifestyle for the first time, but here's where integrating AI into mindfulness routines can be really beneficial.

AI tools provide on-demand, personalized experiences that evolve as you make progress, making mindfulness more adaptable and engaging in the early stages, when you most need help removing barriers such as time constraints. Advanced practitioners can also benefit from discovering innovative ways to take mindfulness to a higher level.

Keep in mind though that AI should be seen as a complement rather than a replacement for traditional mindfulness practices. While AI does offer a source of guidance to give you structure and insights, true mindfulness is an inner journey that lies in the human experience – without total dependence on tech – so you should be 'mindful' of your mindfulness practice in this respect. Whichever way you achieve a more mindful state, your journey should be rooted in self awareness and strike a harmonious balance between solitude and distractions.

Try It Yourself: Build a Personalized Mindfulness Routine

Mindfulness doesn't have to be a separate activity that you set time aside for. It's a practice that you incorporate into your daily routines with tips and prompts on how to maintain a healthy state of mind, no matter what's going on around you. Using ChatGPT can help you discover simple ways to bring mindfulness into everyday moments with a prompt similar to this:

"I want to make mindfulness a habit by integrating it into my daily activities. Can you suggest ways to practice mindfulness while doing routine tasks like commuting, eating, or working?"

To refine the response ChatGPT gives you, try specifying a time of day (morning, evening, work breaks) or a particular focus (stress relief, gratitude, awareness, breathing exercises).

Experiment with different variations and observe how ChatGPT adapts its suggestions. Take note of what resonates with you and give it a go at incorporating it into your routine for a few days to see what works best.

6

CREATIVE USES OF AI

Artificial intelligence is revolutionizing the way creative people work and play – empowering artists, writers, musicians, and filmmakers with tools that really simplify the creative process. Whether you're enhancing photos with AI-powered image editing, composing music with machine learning, or crafting compelling stories with the help of generative AI, these tools are opening doors to a host of new possibilities.

Don't be swayed by nay-sayers repeating the common misconception that AI kills off creativity. That couldn't be further from the truth. AI actually serves to amplify human expression by removing technical barriers, sparking inspiration, and streamlining creative workflows. With AI as a collaborator, individuals of any skill level can experiment, iterate, and refine their work in ways that would have been time-consuming or impossible not so long ago.

In this chapter, we'll explore how AI is reshaping creative fields ranging from visual arts and video production to writing music. You'll discover hands-on ways to leverage AI as a creative partner, whether you're refining an image, composing a song, or bringing a story to life. Let's dive in and uncover how AI can enhance and expand your creative potential.

Give Image Editing a Professional Touch

AI has transformed image editing from a once labor-intensive process into an easy and efficient task. While traditional AI is already widely used to automate enhancements such as color correction and background removal, generative AI plays a key role in more complex tasks such as removing objects, content-aware filling, and realistic image expansions. By generating new pixels that blend seamlessly with existing content, generative AI elevates image editing to a new level of creativity.

Tools such as Adobe Firefly in Photoshop exemplify this shift. You don't even have to move a mouse around anymore as the generative machine learning text-to-image model lets you edit images with text prompts alone, seamlessly adding or removing elements, and generating textures or artistic styles. It's like having a digital assistant with an artistic eye, enhancing photos with minimal effort.

Similarly, Luminar Neo is fully powered by artificial intelligence. It automates adjustments to lighting, contrast, and other factors, adapting to each image's unique characteristics, saving time while ensuring consistent quality that would be very difficult to achieve manually.

Canva Magic Studio has several easy-to-use AI-powered features that combine traditional and generative AI to make image editing more accessible to technophobes. Traditional AI assists with background removal and resizing while generative AI features such as Magic Edit let you modify images by describing changes with text prompts. It's a hybrid approach that gives you creative flexibility while keeping the process intuitive.

While ChatGPT cannot directly edit images, it works well as a support tool by suggesting techniques, explaining AI-powered tools, and helping craft effective prompts for platforms such as Adobe Firefly. With it you can describe an image you want to enhance and ChatGPT will recommend specific edits such as exposure adjustments or vignette effects. In this regard, ChatGPT is a valuable resource if you're a beginner wanting to explore image editing techniques without having to master complex software. With AI handling the technical details, you are free to focus on your creative vision.

Table 14 AI Tools for Image Editing

	ChatGPT	Adobe Firefly	Canva Magic Studio	Luminar Neo
Type of AI	Generative AI	Generative AI	Traditional AI + Generative AI	Traditional AI + Generative AI
Free Version	Yes - Provides editing guidance & prompt tips	Yes - Limited generative editing & fills	Yes - Basic AI edits & templates	No
Paid Version	Yes - Offers advanced AI prompt crafting	Yes - Full access to generative tools	Yes - More AI editing & generative tools	Yes - Full AI-powered image enhancements and generative
Strengths	Guides users on AI tools, suggests edits & workflows	Seamless AI-based object addition, removal & content fill	Quick AI-powered background, object edits, and effects	Fast, realistic photo enhancement and seamless object removal
Weaknesses	Cannot directly edit images, only provides AI guidance	Limited free features, requires subscription for full AI tools	Less precision for complex AI-based edits, mainly for quick fixes	Primarily focused on photo editing, lacking broader creative features
Best Used For	Learning & AI-assisted image guidance	AI-enhanced photo refinements, inspiring creative projects	Quick & easy AI-based image adjustments	Professional photo enhancement and retouching for natural results

Note: The information provided is based on available data as of March 2025 and may be subject to change.

Cutting out image backgrounds is no longer a painstaking process of carefully selecting the parts you want cropped with automatic background removal features and color correction made possible with AI. If you want to isolate subjects in a photo taken at a crowded event, AI tools can achieve this in seconds with great precision. These image editing features free you from laborious manual editing, making it easy to experiment with, and it doesn't matter if you make a mistake when everything is easily undoable.

As mentioned earlier, AI isn't killing off creativity. It's here to enhance the creative process in a collaborative approach with the artist. To maximize

AI in image editing, you should balance automation with manual adjustments by letting AI handle many of the technical tasks while you maintain human oversight, ensuring edits align with your creative vision. Start with AI for basic enhancements, then refine results manually to maintain image quality. Pay attention to details such as sharpness and texture, which AI may not fully capture. With this blend of AI efficiency and human artistry, you can create images that are polished and professional in a short time. By embracing AI as a collaborative tool, you unlock new creative possibilities and elevate your visual content.

Try It Yourself: Enhance Your Image with AI

Now let's get creative with ChatGPT by generating a prompt to enhance one of your digital photos. Find a photo of a sunset or similar scene that you want to make the colors pop and add a dreamy vibe to. You could ask something like this:

"How can I enhance a sunset beach photo to make it more vibrant and give it a surreal feel?"

Once you have your prompt, head over to the free version of Adobe Firefly, upload a photo of a beach at sunset, and see what it can do with the suggestions. Try playing around with different settings to adjust the lighting, mood, or even the texture of the sky. It's all about experimenting and seeing what fits your vision.

- How did Firefly change the feel of the photo?
- Was there an adjustment that surprised you in a good way?
- What's something new you discovered about how AI can enhance images that you hadn't thought of before?

Create Visual Masterpieces

AI has become a powerful creative tool for modern artists seeking new ways to express themselves. With tools such as DeepArt you can transform a simple photo into a masterpiece inspired by Van Gogh's *Starry Night* or Picasso's Cubist works.

DeepArt uses a process called artistic style transfer to apply the aesthetics of one image to another, creating striking artistic blends with endless possibilities. It's great for letting artists explore styles and concepts they might not have considered otherwise.

DALL-E is an AI Image generator with an extensive selection of more than 100 models and styles that's available to subscribers of the paid version of ChatGPT. It can create surreal images for you just from text prompts. If you type in a prompt such as "a dreamscape with a floating castle", you'll see a vivid image quickly materialize. DALL-E can do this because it understands and visualizes ideas, enabling artists to explore the abstract and fantastical with ease. It doesn't just replicate styles. It creates new ones, pushing the boundaries of digital art even further.

Ideogram is another text-to-image model that also harnesses generative AI to produce images from typed prompts, offering unique visuals tailored to user input. The platform MidJourney follows a similar approach, generating high-quality, imaginative artwork from natural language descriptions. Known for stunning artistic renditions, MidJourney has become a favorite among digital creators experimenting with new ideas and styles.

ChatGPT itself provides an intriguing entry point for beginners exploring artistic endeavors for the first time. Although ChatGPT is mainly a text tool, and generally can't actually create or manipulate images for you, it is an excellent resource for conceptualizing visual projects by generating descriptions and prompts for artists. It can also suggest themes, elements, or ideas to incorporate into artwork – sparking inspiration while bridging digital and traditional art in exciting new ways.

Table 15 AI Tools for Image Generation

	ChatGPT	DeepArt	DALL-E	Ideogram	Midjourney
Type of AI	Generative AI	Generative AI	Generative AI	Generative AI	Generative AI
Free Version	Yes - Basic text generation prompts	Yes - Limited image styles & output	Yes - Limited daily generations	Yes - Limited image prompts	No
Paid Version	Yes - Enhanced image prompts & features	Yes - Unlimited styles & output quality	Yes - More generations & higher quality	Yes - Expanded prompt features & image quality	Yes - Full access to AI-powered tools & outputs
Strengths	Great for brainstorming & text-to-image generation	Excels at transforming photos into artwork with unique styles	Generates vivid, creative, and surreal images from text	Quick generation of unique images from text prompts	High-quality artistic images with great detail
Weaknesses	Limited image generation capabilities beyond text input	Slow processing and fewer style options available	Free version has restricted features and output	Text-based prompts limit more complex visual creation	Limited free trial and slower processing times
Best Used For	Concept development, brainstorming, and simple visual ideas	Transforming photographs into diverse artistic styles	Creating imaginative, surreal visuals from textual descriptions	Quickly creating simple, personalized images from prompts	Creating detailed and high-quality artistic designs

Note: The information provided is based on available data as of March 2025 and may be subject to change.

Outside the digital media realm, AI can collaborate with conventional artists using traditional art techniques to help them visualize their work in new ways. An AI assistant can analyze your sketches and offer suggestions for complementary colors or balanced layouts. It can even add AI-generated textures, enhancing depth and detail that might otherwise take hours to refine, allowing artists to focus on their vision while AI manages the technical adjustments.

AI is also transforming how we experience art; in a shift from a passive viewing experience to an interactive encounter. Artists are now using AI to create interactive installations that respond to movement or environmental changes. This form of augmented reality art powered by AI overlays digital creations onto the real world, blending physical and virtual spaces to create dynamic, evolving experiences.

Contemporary artists are increasingly integrating AI into their creative processes, producing works that challenge traditional notions of art. AI-generated art exhibitions are becoming more common, exploring themes of technology, humanity, and the future. These exhibitions often involve collaborations between AI researchers and artists, merging technical expertise with creative vision to produce groundbreaking work. These partnerships exemplify how AI ultimately supports and enhances artistic expression, fostering new forms of creativity and cultural dialogue. And isn't bringing people together what art is all about?

German artist Mario Klingemann is a well-known pioneer in the craft of working with neural networks, code, and algorithms to create thought-provoking art pieces; exploring topics such as identity and perception. His best known exhibitions feature evolving AI-generated portraits meant to challenge viewers by forcing them to consider the relationship between man and machine.

And Turkish-American artist Refik Anadol is pushing the boundaries of art by embedding media arts into architecture with data and machine intelligence in a technique dubbed 'data sculpture'. Harnessing AI as a creative tool, he turns complex information into visual narratives by transforming vast datasets into immersive installations.

*Try It Yourself: Unleash Your Creati*vity with DALL-E

The beauty of using AI in a creative process is that you don't have to be artistically inclined at all. All you need is an idea and DALL-E will transform it into a beautiful, realistic image – no art skills required. Even with the free version of DALL-E, you can turn an image into a stunning visual masterpiece, bringing your imagination to life with just a few words.

Sign-up to the free version of DALL-E and try asking it something like this:

"Can you create a peaceful nature scene with a lake and mountains?"

- What do you think about the image?
- Could you adjust the prompt to change the mood or add new elements, like a different time of day or more wildlife?

Professional Video Production Made Easy

Creating videos with AI might seem like a skill reserved for special effects professionals, especially if you've never worked with video editing software before. However, AI-powered tools are designed to be easily accessible, even for complete beginners. Sure, you'll need a bit of practice to become comfortable but these tools are highly intuitive, allowing you to produce high-quality videos in minutes instead of hours without specialist video editing skills.

There are several AI platforms making video creation easy for beginners such as Synthesia, which is ideal for producing professional videos, complete with AI-generated presenters. Just input the script as text, choose an avatar for your presenter, and let Synthesia generate a realistic video with natural-sounding speech. The results are impressive, giving you the kind of professional quality that's widely used for corporate training, education and marketing videos.

The image art video generator Runway lets you generate videos from text or enhance existing footage with AI effects. The platform gives you a good balance of automation and creative control.

The text-to-video generator Pictory helps content creators turn long-form text such as blog posts into engaging short videos. It automatically selects visuals, generates captions, and adds AI voice overs too.

Pika is an idea-to-video platform that smoothly converts ideas in the form of text and images into dynamic videos, making fast, AI-assisted content creation very simple. None of these tools require expensive equipment or advanced skills – just a willingness to experiment and refine your process.

While ChatGPT doesn't generate videos, it can play a key role in content creation by generating video scripts for presentations, storytelling, and tutorials. It can suggest concepts, outline scenes, draft dialogue, and refine text for AI narrations. ChatGPT can also help you reach more online viewers by optimizing video titles, descriptions, and tags for more exposure on platforms such as YouTube. By combining these different AI tools, you can streamline every stage of video production from the first spark of an idea to final edits and polished production.

Video creation with AI is fun to play around with but it also has fantastic practical applications across diverse industries. Many businesses and educators have switched to using AI-generated videos for onboarding, e-learning, and instructional content. It's quicker, cheaper and much less resource intensive than conventional video production methods.

Table 16 AI Tools for Video Creation

	ChatGPT	Synthesia	Runway	Pictory	Pika
Type of AI	Generative AI	Generative AI	Generative AI	Generative AI	Generative AI
Free Version	Yes - Text-based assistance for video ideas	Yes - Limited features for basic use	Yes - Limited exports and features	No	Yes - Transforms text and images into short videos
Paid Version	Yes - Advanced text assistance and plugins	Yes - Full AI avatars and customization	Yes - More exports, higher resolution, AI tools	Yes - Video generations, templates, AI voice overs	Yes - Advanced features and customization options
Strengths	Great for scriptwriting, structuring, and idea generation	Creates AI avatars with realistic voice synthesis	AI-powered editing, motion effects, and content generation	Transforms text into short, engaging videos with AI automation	Easily turns text and images into videos; user-friendly interface
Weaknesses	Cannot generate videos, only assists with content creation	Limited avatar customization, lacks real video shooting tools	Requires some editing skills for advanced features	Less control over visuals and transitions than manual editors	Limited advanced editing; variable output quality
Best Used For	Generating video scripts and concepts	Professional AI-presenter videos for training	Creative video edits and effects	Converting text into social media videos	Generating quick videos from text and images

Note: The information provided is based on available data as of March 2025 and may be subject to change.

The speed and efficiency of AI-generated videos is also attractive to marketing teams and social media managers who need a quick turnaround on video production for engaging ads, product launches, and brand storytelling.

Bloggers and content creators can also get in on the act to reach a wider audience by repurposing written content into videos. Even personalized video messages for customer engagement are becoming more common with AI. As these tools grow more powerful and accessible, the possibilities continue to expand.

Try It Yourself: Transform Text into Video

Let's try exploring Runway's Text-to-Video feature to generate a short clip from a simple idea. Go to Runway and sign up for a free account. Once logged in, explore the dashboard and locate the Gen-2 model, which allows you to create videos from text prompts or images.

Think of a short, creative scene you'd like to generate. It could be something as simple as:

"A futuristic city glowing under neon lights at night."

Click on the Text-to-Video option and wait for it to generate your video.

- What worked well in your prompt, and what could be improved?
- How could you use this tool for storytelling, social media, or personal projects?

Writing and Storytelling with AI Assistance

When you're staring at a blank page struggling with writer's block, you can get your writing flowing with help from the many AI-powered writing assistants now available.

When it comes to creative writing, AI not only helps you break through writing blocks, it can also inspire new narratives and plots. As such, writers are increasingly adopting AI writing assistants as creative partners, transforming how we approach storytelling. With AI-assisted tools, even the most daunting blank page becomes a canvas of possibilities.

Sudowrite is a non-judgemental writing partner designed with fiction writers in mind, acting as a brainstorming companion that offers plot ideas and character suggestions. It provides the scaffolding to develop your narrative, whether you're crafting a short story or creating an entire fantasy world.

The text-based adventure-story game AI Dungeon takes storytelling even further, allowing you to co-create dynamic adventures in real time, and play the starring role in them. It's the perfect extension for taking gaming to a more creative level and entices fantasy writers who enjoy open-ended storytelling.

If you're new to co-writing with AI, ChatGPT is an accessible starting point. It helps generate content, refine ideas, and develop dialogue. By providing ChatGPT with prompts and context, you can guide it to draft scenes or outline chapters. Its intuitive interface makes it easy for beginners to dive into AI-assisted writing without technical skills.

ChatGPT's versatility supports all kinds of projects, from articles and essays to fiction, making it a valuable tool whenever inspiration is lacking. Over time, collaborating with AI boosts productivity and enhances the quality of your work.

Table 17 AI Tools for Writing and Storytelling

	ChatGPT	Sudowrite	AI Dungeon
Type of AI	Generative AI	Generative AI	Generative AI
Free Version	Yes - Basic AI writing help	No	Yes - Limits on how much you can play
Paid Version	Yes - Advanced text assistance	Yes - Full features	Yes - More powerful AI, fewer restrictions
Strengths	Good for many types of writing, helps with ideas	Great for fiction, suggests plots and characters	Fun for interactive storytelling and roleplaying
Weaknesses	Doesn't help much with structuring long stories	Only good for fiction, not for essays or reports	Can be unpredictable, needs user input to guide
Best Used For	General writing, brainstorming, content drafting	Fiction writing, story expansion, character ideas	Interactive storytelling, game-like narratives

Note: The information provided is based on available data as of March 2025 and may be subject to change.

Beyond using AI as a co-writing tool for generating ideas, you can enlist AI to explore new possibilities and push storytelling boundaries with alternative endings or unexpected plot twists to ensure you keep stories fresh and engaging.

With AI's ability to generate diverse scenarios, it encourages you as a writer to think outside the box, exploring paths you might not have considered. Your protagonist's journey could take a surprising new turn or a mystery could get resolved in an unforeseen way with this kind of collaboration to enrich storytelling and create narratives that surprise and captivate readers.

For the record, we're not talking about using AI tools to do all the writing for you. We're talking about getting help with your own ideas and having the ability to expand on them in a free-flowing way where you are ultimately in control of the narrative.

Setting the scene and creating characters is a really useful way writers can use AI to get inspiration by generating story elements they can build on. Using an AI-generated character profile can explore a hero's or villain's fears, desires, and quirks, adding layers of depth.

Similarly, AI-generated setting descriptions transport readers into immersive worlds, which could be anything from a bustling market filled with colorful stalls to a serene forest where sunlight filters through the canopy – vivid details that bring stories to life, engaging readers' senses in your storytelling.

With characters and settings established, you can go even further by asking AI to suggest character arcs that add depth and complexity to your narratives. With AI-generated profiles you can weave in important story-telling aspects such as background, motivations, and conflicts to make characters more lifelike and relatable.

Dialogue generation is another strong feature in AI writing tools, helping you craft realistic interactions that reflect authentic speech patterns and cultural nuances. This is particularly useful in dialogue-heavy scenes or when creating diverse characters, ensuring authenticity in storytelling.

Overall, collaborating with AI in writing projects opens new creative avenues and accelerates the process from start to finish, allowing writers to refine content quickly and stay focused on weaving an enthralling story.

For writing workshops, AI can act as a brainstorming partner, helping groups explore new ideas and bring fresh elements into the writing process, enhancing the overall story. You just let AI handle the repetitive tasks and give suggestions while you maintain creative control to ensure the final result is what you envisioned.

Try It Yourself: Expand and Enrich a Story with AI

Try this exercise to see for yourself how AI can help to overcome writer's block by expanding your ideas and enhancing descriptions.

Open ChatGPT and Type a prompt such as:

"A mysterious figure appeared in the dark alley. Can you expand on this scene, making it more suspenseful and adding details about the setting and the figure?"

Once ChatGPT responds, take a moment to read through the continuation.

- Does the AI bring something unexpected to the scene?
- Did it enhance the atmosphere or introduce new ideas that you could use in your story?

AI-Driven Music and Audio Production

Just as writers and artists are benefitting from co-creating with AI assistance, amateur music makers are now pushing out professionally made tracks without having to know a single note or play an actual instrument. With software such as AIVA, Suno, and Mubert, almost anyone can compose original music or command an entire orchestra thanks to the latest AI advancements.

The music generation assistant AIVA analyzes musical patterns to create compositions in genres from classical to punk rock and jazz, letting you experiment with a wealth of different styles. Whether you're crafting anything from a simple melody to a symphony, AIVA bridges the gap between inspiration and realization.

Harmonizing melodies is no longer an issue for those of us that are a bit tone deaf, either, with AI simplifying the melody-making process by suggesting complementary notes and chords, guiding the creative process with precision, even if you don't have the best ears for it.

Suno is one of the latest generative artificial intelligence music creation programs helping budding songwriters find their niche. It's designed to generate realistic songs that combine vocals and instrumentation. You just have to give it some text prompts to come up with lyrics, instrumentals, and vocals to end up with a fully produced song in a matter of minutes. The fine tuning and juggling around may take a while longer but using Suno makes creating music almost effortless by offering quick inspiration to explore new sounds.

Mubert Music Generator specializes in creating royalty-free music by blending generative AI with user input to create algorithmically generated soundscapes, making it a go-to platform for content creators and streamers wanting to avoid potential copyright strikes.

Table 18 AI Tools for Music Generation

	ChatGPT	**Suno**	**AIVA**	**Mubert**
Type of AI	Generative AI	Generative AI	Generative AI	Generative AI
Free Version	Yes - Text-based lyric & music prompts	Yes - Generates full songs with limits	Yes - Limited compositions and export options	Yes - Generates short AI music loops
Paid Version	Yes - More advanced creative control	Yes - More songs & better audio quality	Yes - Unlimited compositions and commercial use	Yes - Yes, longer, custom AI-generated music
Strengths	Great for lyric generation & brainstorming compositions	Complete song creation incl. lyrics, instruments, vocals	Creates structured musical scores, good for compositions	Generates royalty-free music in real-time, AI-driven
Weaknesses	No direct music/audio creation, only text-based support	Limited free use, AI-generated vocals may lack nuance	Mostly digital output, lacks full instrumental production	Limited free customization, AI-generated music may repeat
Best Used For	Lyric & composition brainstorming	Full song creation from text prompts	Composing structured instrumental music, like soundtracks	Background music for content creators

Note: The information provided is based on available data as of March 2025 and may be subject to change.

AI in audio production is also helping podcasters make polished presentations with platforms such as ElevenLabs and Descript, which turn written scripts into engaging voice overs in a variety of tones and styles. It's a speedy way to experiment with a variety of voices to pick the best one for a podcast that resonates with their audience.

Combining these tools in each of their specialist fields can produce great music and soundtracks at lightning speed compared to the arduous process of getting people in front of microphones and eliminating annoying background noises, clicks and hisses, which can be a considerably time-consuming part of the post-production process. Not anymore though, when you combine Descript with Adobe Podcast, for example. Pairing up these apps simplifies editing with automatic transcription, making it easy to cut fillers or rearrange segments.

With Mubert you can generate appropriate background music for the podcast mood and theme to give them a consistent auditory identity.

Even for beginners, ChatGPT is a handy support tool for music production. It can help you brainstorm lyrics and structure compositions, helping translate ideas into harmonious sounds. For creative inspiration, ChatGPT suggests content ideas, topics, and episode outlines.

Table 19 AI Tools for Audio Production

	ChatGPT	ElevenLabs	Descript	Adobe Podcast
Type of AI	Generative AI	Generative AI	Traditional AI + Generative AI	Traditional AI
Free Version	Yes - Text-based script & dialogue generation	Yes - Limited AI voice generation & cloning	Yes - Basic transcription & text-to-speech	Yes - Basic noise reduction & enhancement
Paid Version	Yes - More advanced creative control	Yes - More voices, higher quality, more usage	Yes - Advanced editing, overdubbing, AI voice cloning	Yes - Premium noise reduction, studio-quality enhancement
Strengths	Great for scriptwriting, dialogue, & content ideas	Realistic AI voices, voice cloning, & multilingual support	Strong transcription, overdubbing, & AI-driven editing	Studio-quality noise reduction & speech enhancement
Weaknesses	No direct audio creation, only text-based support	Limited free use, AI voices may sound robotic	Manual adjustments needed for precise editing	No AI voice generation, only enhances existing audio
Best Used For	Scriptwriting & brainstorming podcast/audio content	Generating AI voice overs & custom voice cloning	Editing podcasts & videos with AI-powered tools	Improving audio quality for podcasts & recordings

Note: The information provided is based on available data as of March 2025 and may be subject to change.

As well as helping to create music and podcasts, AI has made audio editing a lot easier, refining and enhancing sound quality with advanced algorithms that remove background noise while preserving natural tone. With these noise-reduction tools, creators can devote their attention to crafting content without worrying about distracting technical issues.

AI also excels in sound design so you can craft immersive audio experiences to evoke specific moods. With a few prompts, AI can transport your listeners to a serene beach, a bustling city or the middle of a steamy jungle.

Music production and mixing become more intuitive, too, with AI streamlining complex tasks for you. Automated mixing ensures track volumes are harmoniously balanced, while mastering tools optimize audio levels for various playback environments. AI can even analyze each track's nuances, suggesting adjustments to enhance overall sound much like a professional producer – helping you produce mainstream-quality music without having any technical skills yourself – democratizing music production so that anyone can put out well-polished tracks.

As machine-composed albums gain traction, AI music production is challenging traditional notions of authorship, creating a bit of controversy in their wake, but ultimately empowering musicians and audio technicians with a creative partner that's always willing and able to adapt to your vision. It's clear that AI's influence on audio production will only grow and continue opening new artistic frontiers.

Try It Yourself: Create Your Own Music

Let's put AI to work and create a song with Suno – no musical experience required!

Sign up to the Suno free version and describe your song. Think about the mood, genre, or theme you want. For example, you can ask for *"an energetic pop song about chasing dreams"* Or *"a calm acoustic melody about a rainy afternoon"*.

Let Suno create your track, and, once it's ready, listen back carefully.

- How well do the lyrics fit the theme?
- How did it feel to create music with AI?
- Did it spark any creative ideas for you?

Make a Difference with Your Review

Unlock the Power of Learning Together

> "When you learn, teach. When you get, give."
>
> Maya Angelou

People who share what they've learned with others can make a real, long-lasting impact. So, let's make a difference together!

Would you help someone just like you – curious about how to best use AI in their daily life, but not sure where to begin?

My mission is to make learning about AI easy for everyone. I believe AI should be used responsibly in ways that make a positive impact on the world and help humans feel more empowered.

But to reach more people who want to learn, I need your help.

Most people pick books based on what others say about them. So, I'm asking you to help a fellow AI beginner by leaving a review.

It costs nothing and takes less than a minute but could change someone's AI learning journey. Your review could help...

...one more student discover the amazing world of AI. ...one more teacher bring exciting lessons to their classroom or offer more personalized support. ...one more parent show their child how to be responsible digital citizens in an AI world. ...one more curious mind explore new ideas. ...one more future creator build something awesome that helps people.

To make a difference, simply scan the QR code below and leave a review:

https://geni.us/euJNPNB

If you love helping others learn cool stuff about technology that matters, you're my kind of person. Thank you for being part of this learning journey!

Sarah T. Rowan

PART III: BOOST YOUR CONFIDENCE IN USING AI

7

BUILD A FRAMEWORK FOR AI INTERACTION

If you have a conversation with someone that speaks a different language to you, your intent could be easily lost in translation. The same is true when working with AI, because the way you phrase your prompts directly shapes the responses AI gives you. Understanding how to craft effective prompts, refine your communication, and customize AI to fit your needs makes the difference between the frustration of crossed wires and the joy of being understood.

This chapter will equip you with the skills to confidently transform AI from a tool you use occasionally into a reliable, responsive assistant that works the way you do.

How to Craft Effective AI Prompts

Prompts are at the core of your interactions with AI so to get it working with you effectively, you have to feed it with a query or statement to generate a desired response.

I cannot overstate the importance of crafting precise AI prompts, just as you need to establish a clear method of communication with a non-native speaker, so things don't get lost in translation. Giving AI clear, well-defined prompts helps it understand your requests and respond appropriately to them. So, when you define the scope and context of your questions, do think carefully about what you want to achieve by asking yourself whether you're seeking a specific answer or exploring broader possibilities.

A well-crafted prompt sets the stage for AI to deliver relevant and insightful responses. Ambiguity is the enemy of effective prompting, so avoid vague language that leaves AI guessing your intentions. Instead, use specific keywords that focus AI responses and guide them toward your desired outcome. For instance, instead of saying "Tell me about AI", specify your interest with a more elaborate prompt such as "Explain how AI is used in healthcare for patient diagnostics".

By incorporating context details, you provide AI with the necessary background to tailor its responses to your needs, resulting in more accurate and useful information.

Organization is key when you're structuring AI prompts. Begin with a clear and concise statement that outlines your objective. Include relevant context to help AI understand the situation so it can formulate a response that aligns with your goals.

Be mindful of the language you use and keep it simple. Avoid technical jargon that might confuse AI algorithms. Opt for straightforward terms that convey your message effectively instead. The clearer you make your prompts, the more precise the response from the AI system.

While details in your prompts are important, overloading prompts with unnecessary information is a common pitfall when creating prompts that can hinder the effectiveness of your interactions with AI. Excessive input can overwhelm AI systems and lead to confusion, so focus on the essential elements of your query, distilling your prompt to its core components.

To enhance your ability to craft effective AI prompts, consider three widely used frameworks:

- TAG (Type, Audience, Goal): This method ensures clarity by specifying the type of response needed, the target audience, and the overall goal. For example, *"Write a beginner-friendly explanation of blockchain technology for high school students"* ensures that AI tailors the response accordingly.

- RTF (Role, Task, Format): This framework helps structure prompts by specifying the AI's role, then defining the task, and then outlining the desired format of the response. For example, *"You are a financial advisor. Provide a short explanation of investment diversification in bullet points"*.

- RACEF (Role, Action, Context, Example, Format): This more detailed approach refines prompts by incorporating role, required action, background context, an example for guidance, and the desired format. For instance, *"As a nutritionist, create a personalized weekly meal plan for a vegetarian athlete, including protein-rich meal options and a daily calorie target"*.

Moment of Reflection: Improve Your Prompts

As you explore AI prompting in any of the areas introduced in Part II of this book, practice crafting prompts for different scenarios. Try, for example, planning a vacation itinerary like the one suggested in Chapter 3, then create a series of alternative prompts to guide AI in generating suggestions. Reflect on the clarity and conciseness of your prompts and how AI responds.

Consider how refining your prompts might lead to more accurate and actionable outcomes. If you try this exercise with different scenarios, you'll soon improve your prompting skills and gain a deeper understanding of effective AI interaction.

Enhance Communication with AI

Communicating effectively with AI is much like having a conversation with a friend. There's a mutual understanding between you based on clarity, patience, and an understanding of the nuances involved. Surprisingly, one of the most effective ways to enhance this dialogue is to simply use a conversational tone when interacting with AI systems.

Taking a natural approach to your interactions actually helps AI better understand your intent. When you phrase your queries as if you're speaking to a real person, AI can often provide more relevant and accurate responses. For instance, instead of issuing a command like *"Retrieve weather data"*, try making it a more conversational question by rephrasing it to *"What's the weather like today?"*.

You'll find that this subtle shift in tone can significantly improve the quality of the interaction, making it more engaging and effective. I even add 'please' and 'thank you', not because AI needs it, but because it makes the conversation feel more natural to me!

Providing feedback to AI is crucial for refining communication between the two of you and helps AI adapt and improve over time. Your feedback could be through explicit ratings, comments, or implicit signals such as repeatedly using suggested outputs.

When you rate an AI response, you're teaching the system what works and what doesn't. Suggesting improvements helps developers fine-tune algorithms, ensuring future interactions better align with user expectations. This feedback loop enhances AI's utility and reliability, making it increasingly effective over time.

You should also approach your AI conversations with realistic expectations. AI is indeed powerful but it has limitations, especially in understanding nuanced conversations. While it excels at processing data and providing factual answers, AI may well struggle with processing emotions or sarcasm. Recognizing these limits helps manage expectations and avoid frustration.

Keep in mind that AI is a tool designed to assist, not replace human intuition or emotional intelligence. If you have a good understanding of its strengths and weaknesses, you'll be able to use AI effectively to complement your decision-making.

In automated customer service roles, chatbots can efficiently handle most generic questions and some basic complaints, allowing human agents to focus on complex issues, but there are limitations. The success of AI chatbots depends on effective communication. Using conversational language and providing feedback improves interactions, leading to better customer experiences.

In a more creative context, AI-assisted brainstorming can generate ideas and expand possibilities. In this case, keeping an open dialogue with AI allows you and other users to refine projects and explore new concepts with increasing ease.

In both customer service and creative contexts, communicating successfully with AI is a balance of human input and AI output. By engaging with AI with realistic expectations and giving it constructive feedback, you foster productive collaboration that expertly enhances personal and professional tasks.

AI is a powerful ally, but it requires guidance to reach its full potential. Thoughtful communication unlocks new levels of efficiency and creativity, making AI an integral part of daily interactions.

Try It Yourself: Does it Make a Difference?

Try running the same query in ChatGPT twice – once as a direct command and once using a more conversational tone.

Example using a command:

"Summarize the benefits of AI in education."

Example using a conversational tone:

"Hey! Could you please explain how AI is improving education? I'm curious about the benefits."

- Compare the responses. Do they feel different?
- Is one more detailed or engaging than the other?

Customize AI Interactions for Personal Use

The longer you work with an AI tool, the more intuitive it becomes as it adapts to your needs. With a few tweaks you can adjust notification settings to get instant alerts for urgent matters or be less intrusive, which is handy when working across different time zones.

Language isn't an issue either, because most AI assistants are multilingual, making it easy to navigate your personalized dashboard to work and communicate across borders.

Through your dashboard you can organize information, prioritize task management, get the news and social media updates you want, and much more.

For recurring tasks such as making grocery lists, workout routines, or project timelines, you can quickly set up custom templates to make them more efficient.

On fitness apps you can key in personal metrics for customized workout plans that you can adapt as you progress. Or, if you're an avid reader, you can discover new books by getting AI to generate reading lists that match favorite genres and authors.

These are just a few of the ways AI can be tailored to your individual needs. As you explore these customization options, AI becomes a more supportive and integral part of daily life, making it simpler and more structured.

Try It Yourself: Personalize Your ChatGPT Experience

To make ChatGPT work better for you, just tell it how you want it to respond to you. Think about whether you'd prefer short, concise answers or detailed explanations, and whether you'd like formal and structured responses or a more casual approach with a friendly tone.

Use the prompt below to tell ChatGPT your preferences:

"I'd like you to adjust how you respond to better match my preferences. Please keep responses [concise/detailed], *use a* [formal/casual] *tone, and focus on topics related to* [list interests, e.g., fitness, technology, productivity]. *Also, please* [mention any specific requests, such as summarizing information before explaining it further]. *"*

Test whether ChatGPT understood the task by asking it a question about your interests.

- How well did ChatGPT's response match your preferences?
- What adjustments would make it even better?

To make ChatGPT remember your preferences, customize the settings in your profile (top-right corner on desktop or in the settings menu on mobile devices). Select 'Customize ChatGPT' and enter details about your interests and response preferences.

8

TROUBLESHOOT COMMON AI CHALLENGES

We've all imagined a scenario in the near future where AI will somehow outsmart us and take over the world, bringing humanity to its knees. It's a great movie plot, but like anything out of Hollywood, it's an exaggeration. While AI has incredible capabilities, it does have boundaries which are often misunderstood.

The Truth About AI Capabilities and Limitations

At its core, AI does not have a true understanding of itself and its environment. It isn't conscious like us. It operates by analyzing patterns in data provided by humans, making predictions rather than 'thinking' in the way we do.

AI does nothing more than process that information through machine learning algorithms and neural networks. It relies on us, the users, to provide it with quality data. Any bias or inaccuracies in AI's output come down to our ability to use our discernment.

And that's why AI isn't a replacement for human creativity. While AI can generate content, it doesn't have the ability to innovate beyond its training data. Our human creativity comes from emotions, experiences, and intuition – elements that AI does not have and cannot replicate. It can expertly mimic styles based on existing data, enhancing creativity but not entirely replacing it.

On the other hand, AI does excel at automating specific tasks such as pattern recognition, which can be used to our benefit in many different ways. In a healthcare setting, for example, AI can assist doctors by detecting patterns in scans and X-rays, but the doctor makes the final diagnosis based on their experience, intuition and real-world wisdom. So no matter how smart AI is, it remains a collaborative tool; not a replacement for a medical professional.

No matter how we use AI, it does not make complex decisions on its own. It relies only on the predefined rules and data that we give it, so it always needs human oversight.

That's also why AI isn't a replacement for the creativity of authors. When you use AI as a writing assistant, it can indeed help you with ideas, grammar, and things like plot suggestions – as we have seen in Chapter 6 – yet it lacks the creative capacity of human depth and emotional resonance. Ultimately the writer's voice and vision shape the story.

To maximize the benefits of using AI, be realistic about these limitations. Establish a clear vision of your goals and clearly define how you want AI to help you achieve them, always keeping in mind that AI is a tool for decision-making, not a replacement.

Moment of Reflection: Your Interactions with AI so Far

Reflect on your experiences with AI so far.

Have you encountered situations where AI exceeded or fell short of your expectations?

Consider how your understanding of AI's capabilities influences your interactions with it to help you set realistic expectations when using it.

Useful Strategies to Overcome Technical Barriers

If you're just starting out exploring AI tools, you may encounter a few frustrating teething problems but there are always simple solutions.

Many AI applications such as chatbots, image generators, and writing assistants, are available online so you'll have to sign up for an account to get started.

Browser compatibility and platform limitations are some of the issues you might have when registering an account. If you're using an obscure browser, try switching to Chrome, Firefox, or Edge.

If your verification code doesn't arrive after signing up, check your spam folders or try using a different phone number.

High demand from a high volume of users can sometimes make AI chatbots unresponsive. Try waiting a few minutes or refreshing the page.

If AI's responses seem off-topic, try rephrasing your request or breaking it into smaller parts to improve accuracy.

Many free AI tools have daily usage limits, so if your access is restricted, you might have to upgrade to a paid plan.

If you're using AI-powered creativity tools such as image and video generators, you might experience slow processing times, especially during peak hours. If the output quality doesn't match expectations, try adjusting resolution settings and refining your prompts to be more specific.

As you usually have to access AI online, you might experience connectivity issues. Try solutions such as restarting your router, disabling conflicting browser extensions, or checking platform status pages to diagnose the problem. When in doubt, head for community forums, support pages, and video tutorials offering troubleshooting guidance from experts.

With a bit of patience and persistence, you'll soon get over these teething problems and begin benefitting from AI-powered applications.

Humanize AI with Lateral Thinking and Creativity

If you're a musician composing a new song, AI can go so far as generating melodies, suggesting chord progressions, and even creating harmonies based on vast datasets of existing music, but AI won't be creating any hits by itself. Without your human input of emotions and the ability to bend or break the rules, a song created by AI remains purely mechanical and expressionless.

Only human creativity can transform AI from a tool into a collaborator. AI can handle repetitive tasks and provide data-driven suggestions, yet it is our creativity that breathes life into the final product.

AI usually approaches problem-solving with vertical thinking, meaning it follows logical, structured paths based on existing data. That's why it's very good at recognizing patterns, optimizing solutions, and making predictions.

However, most of the problems we want AI to help us solve are multifaceted issues that cannot be fully resolved with AI's vertical thinking alone. They need the kind of lateral thinking that can explore all manner of possible outcomes, like a mind map, to make the kind of unconventional connections that only human minds can make through intuition and experience.

For example, if AI is trained to generate advertising slogans, it will suggest ones based on successful campaigns from the past. It may refine language and maximize engagement metrics, but it won't necessarily produce a truly fresh idea.

Humans though can take inspiration from unrelated sources such as a poem, a personal experience, or an unusual wordplay to craft something entirely new.

The same goes for using an AI image generator to create artwork. The AI may provide technically polished results, but you as a user can push creativity further by blending multiple images, adding unexpected elements, or using AI-generated textures in unexpected ways.

Likewise, when using AI for brainstorming – for writing, content creation, or even home decor ideas – the key is not to accept AI's first suggestion but to build upon it, remixing and adapting its output in ways AI itself wouldn't 'think' to do.

Whatever creative process you're using AI to help you with, this synergy between human creativity and AI demonstrates that AI is not a replacement for human ingenuity. It is an amplifier.

By embracing AI as a creative collaborator, we unlock a future where technology enhances human imagination rather than constraining it. True innovation comes not from AI alone, but from our ability to think beyond its patterns, break its structures, and create something entirely new.

Try It Yourself: Employ AI as Your Creative Partner

Before partnering with AI for a big creative project, see how it can help you with a small challenge that requires you to add your own twist of originality. Try asking ChatGPT for help making a real-life decision about something simple such as planning a surprise for a friend, refreshing your wardrobe, or choosing a weekend activity. Then take a moment to assess its response.

Does it feel useful but predictable?

Now push it further. Ask for an unexpected alternative, something completely different from its first idea.

If AI suggests a dinner-and-movie night, could you turn it into a themed adventure?

If it recommends a simple outfit update, could you elevate it into a standout look by adding your personal touch?

Mix ideas, break patterns, and make it personal.

On reflection:

- Did AI's logic give you a solid base?
- Where did your own creativity make it more exciting?

Notice how AI can offer inspiration, but it's your lateral thinking that makes the result truly original.

Embrace Human-AI Collaboration

As we've seen, AI is most powerful when it complements human intelligence and lateral thinking rather than replacing it. Whatever industry you're in, whether it's education or finance, AI is an expansion toolkit that lets your innovation flourish with its personalization features. You provide the context and strategy while the AI processes the complex data.

Concerns about AI replacing jobs are natural, but history shows that transformative technologies create more opportunities than they eliminate. When the internet emerged, many feared disruption, yet it revolutionized work, communication, and innovation. Before then, the same happened with personal computers, which were once a niche, but are now essential in nearly every profession.

AI is just the next step in this evolution of our partnership with technology. In that sense, AI is not a competitor but a partner, amplifying human capabilities and expanding possibilities. By embracing this collaboration, we can drive personal and professional growth, ensuring AI remains a tool for empowerment rather than disruption.

Now let's explore how AI can integrate into daily life to unlock new levels of efficiency and innovation.

Moment of Reflection: Your AI Perspective

Take a moment to reflect on your journey through this book so far.

- How did you perceive AI before starting this book?
- How do you perceive AI now after trying it out?

Consider the ways AI can support you in your personal and professional life. Has this new perspective influenced how you plan to interact with AI moving forward?

Jot down your thoughts and observations. You might be surprised by how much your perspective has evolved.

9

HOW TO BALANCE EFFICIENCY AND ETHICS

You and a friend could use the same ride-sharing app and travel the same distance only to realize later that one of you paid more than the other for the exact same ride.

So why did you have to pay different amounts?

The ride-sharing app likely used AI-driven dynamic pricing to make real-time adjustments to each fare based on various factors such as demand, location, and even your personal data.

While these additional insights make the app more efficient, and give you a more personalized experience, they can impact the app's ability to provide a fair and transparent service across the board.

With AI systems now making life-changing decisions for tasks such as screening job applications or granting access to resources, we must be hyper vigilant to ensure inclusivity by preventing a potential bias from creeping in.

Keeping these societal and ethical implications in mind helps us use AI responsibly so that it benefits everyone equally.

Avoid Ethical Dilemmas When Using AI

We rely heavily on AI for transparency and accountability, but we should never take it for granted. When AI systems lack transparency, they can become a Pandora's Box of complications, making it difficult to assess their fairness or accuracy.

As you are ultimately responsible for any data used or produced by AI on your behalf, you must understand how AI systems make decisions. As such, laying down ethical guidelines is essential for ensuring transparency when AI influences decisions for things such as loans, recruitment, and medical care.

A lack of accountability in this regard can lead to high-stakes ethical dilemmas. Healthcare algorithms used to determine access to critical care programs, for example, have been known to discriminate against certain ethnic groups. The bias arose from the AI relying on historical cost data rather than individual patient's actual health needs – a bias that unintentionally reinforced systemic inequalities.

Additionally, systems protected by inadequate security can be compromised and reputations destroyed when AI systems collect and infer sensitive personal data without explicit consent.

Social media platforms, for example, use AI to analyze online behavior and predict personal traits such as political views or mental health status. Protect your privacy when using them by regularly reviewing your app settings to control the data you share. Also be cautious about any personal information you disclose online.

Misinformation is spreading like wildfire these days with a proliferation of AI-generated content such as 'deepfake' videos and articles created by

AI that are used to manipulate public perception and opinion, making it increasingly challenging to distinguish fact from fiction.

To prevent the spread of false narratives, you should always verify the credibility of AI-generated news and cross-check the information with trusted sources before sharing it.

Really though, the benefits of using AI far outweigh these overblown sensational stories, which we should always read with discernment and put into perspective. After all, AI is like any other tool that we use to make life easier; it depends how you use it. You can use a hammer to fix a house or tear it down. We just have to use those tools responsibly for the purpose they are intended.

AI-driven recommendations ranging from news articles to product suggestions often reinforce biases and limit exposure to diverse perspectives. To counteract this, you should diversify your information sources and critically evaluate algorithmic recommendations rather than passively accepting them.

Supporting services with clear transparency policies and engaging in discussions about AI ethics helps promote responsible technology. Ethical AI isn't just about how it's built. It's about how we interact with and shape its influence in society. By questioning, verifying, and advocating for responsible AI, we can ensure it serves humanity fairly and with integrity.

Moment of Reflection: Using AI Responsibly

Think about a generative AI tool you've used such as ChatGPT or an AI image generator.

- How does it handle your information?

- Does it save what you type or create?
- Are its responses always accurate, or have you noticed mistakes?

If the AI generates something misleading, take one simple step to use AI more responsibly by double-checking facts. Be mindful of privacy settings and think critically about AI-generated content before sharing them.

Understand Bias and Fairness

Bias is a key issue that you may encounter with AI. It's like an invisible force that can skew results, often without you realizing. Bias creeps in because AI models learn from datasets, some of which may reflect historical prejudices. For example, if a facial recognition system is trained mostly on images from certain ethnic backgrounds, it may struggle to identify individuals from other ethnic groups.

Such an unintentional bias isn't necessarily a technical issue. It just reflects the data that the AI was trained on, but biased data leads to biased decisions with real-world consequences, such as misidentifications in security or exclusion from services.

To this end, developers are continually trying to iron out bias issues through improved datasets and audits, but you as a user must recognize where bias might creep in.

Biases can be trivial, affecting small things such as social media feeds or product recommendations when you're shopping online, because the output was based on biased data rather than your own actual preferences. But a bias in scenarios such as recruitment, where an AI-powered hiring tool or resume scanner may not assess all candidates fairly can have far more serious, life-changing consequences for candidates. Likewise, if you're applying for a job, AI-driven hiring tools may prioritize certain keywords that don't reflect your actual experience.

Bias in AI results can also affect credit approvals, and even impact medical diagnosis, so any professional using AI assistance should scrutinize its responses, cross-check outputs with other sources, and develop an understanding of potential biases instead of just accepting results at face value.

If an AI recommendation seems off, trust your gut instincts and look into the data it was trained on. Consider who benefits from these results, and whether it favors certain outcomes.

Be hyper critical in your approach, especially if you're using AI for the first time. Compare the responses you get with reputable sources and expert opinions. Take time to learn how AI makes decisions, even through simplified explanations, so you can interpret its recommendations more effectively, which you can do by reading AI transparency reports.

You can avoid bias feedback loops by varying your queries. When using AI-powered search engines or recommendation systems, actively seek different perspectives by rephrasing queries, searching in multiple languages, or manually exploring sources outside algorithmic priorities.

When using AI-generated content tools, experiment with different prompts to see how responses change and whether certain perspectives are consistently left out. As you become more familiar with an AI tool, you can develop strategies to use it more effectively or work around biases.

As users of AI, we have a duty to push for transparency and fairness. If you do come across bias results in these critical areas, speak up to create greater awareness. You can do this by providing feedback or contacting customer support, as well as discussing AI ethics publicly to encourage companies to address these issues.

The more we contribute, the more equitable AI systems become.

Try It Yourself: Test ChatGPT for Bias

Let's put ChatGPT to the test for bias with a quick experiment. This simple test helps you recognize AI bias and fine-tune how you use ChatGPT to get the most balanced and useful results.

Ask a question twice but phrase it slightly differently each time. First, ask a broad question such as *"What are the most common leadership qualities?"*.

Then, rephrase the question slightly, adding a specific demographic detail, such as *"What are the most common leadership qualities in women?"*.

Compare the responses to see if they differ.

- Are male leaders described differently from female leaders?
- If there's a difference, what does that tell you about AI's potential biases?

Think about how such biases could affect hiring recommendations, career advice, or media portrayals generated by AI so you can consider rewording your queries to get a fuller picture when you use AI in a real-life situation.

Keep Your Personal Data Safe in the Age of AI

AI systems can be targeted in cyber attacks, so protecting your personal data is crucial when using them. Data privacy is more than shielding information from hackers. You should understand the risks of data breaches and unauthorized access, even when you're dealing with reputable companies, which can inadvertently expose sensitive information, potentially opening you up to identity theft and financial losses.

Did you hear about the Cambridge Analytica scandal? The political consulting firm Cambridge Analytica used AI to harvest data about millions of Facebook users, without their consent, in order to influence voter behavior. The scandal highlighted the need for users to be aware of online privacy issues, but it also had the benefit of bringing about sweeping regulatory changes to keep private data safe. Facebook faced big fines, and was forced to implement stricter data access policies for third-party apps.

The consulting firm was capitalizing on the new-found ability of AI-powered applications to use data to improve their services. It was a very public lesson on how to manage AI properly in this evolutionary process.

Understanding how AI learns from your interactions – whether through voice commands, search history, or app usage – helps you make informed decisions about using it. Check your privacy settings, limit data sharing, and regularly review app permissions to stay in control of your data.

AI surveillance adds another layer to privacy concerns. Facial recognition is now prevalent in airports and retail stores, as well as on some online platforms.

While these measures may be justified for security reasons, how much privacy are you willing to trade for your safety?

Practical steps you can take to protect yourself include disabling facial recognition on social media, limiting location tracking, and supporting policies that promote AI transparency.

In the USA, the UK and the EU, we are somewhat protected by national privacy regulations such as the California Consumer Privacy Act (CCPA) and the EU General Data Protection Regulation (GDPR), which is considered the world standard for ensuring privacy, transparency and user consent.

Developers can use data anonymization and stronger encryption, but you must take responsibility for managing your digital footprint, which you can do by opting out of data tracking, using privacy-focused tools such as virtual private networks (VPNs), and generally being cautious with your personal data.

Using encryption so that only authorized users can access it is a simple but effective security step you can take. Many messaging apps and websites already use encryption, but you can also apply it to files and emails for added security.

Find the privacy settings in any apps you're using and opt out of unnecessary data sharing such as your location and contacts.

Any reputable app should ask you before accessing your private information and give you complete control over what you share. This consent-based data collection is essential for maintaining trust in AI.

App developers can and should use various anonymization techniques to protect your data but you also play a role by staying informed, advocating for stronger privacy standards, and making mindful choices about your AI interactions.

Moment of Reflection: How Safe is Your Data?

Take a moment to think about your online habits. Ask yourself:

- Do you know what personal data AI-powered apps are collecting about you?
- When was the last time you checked or updated your privacy settings?
- If a data breach happened today, what private details could be

exposed?

Jot down one immediate action you can take to improve your privacy such as reviewing app permissions, enabling encryption, or adjusting privacy settings. They're small steps you can take that your future self will thank you for!

Bridge Cultural and Socioeconomic Gaps

Artificial intelligence brings us unprecedented opportunities to preserve cultural heritage and languages for future generations. In a role as a digital guardian, AI can document speech, writing and images of cultures on the brink of extinction.

But at the same time, AI can unintentionally perpetuate cultural biases, when its systems are trained on datasets reflecting dominant perspectives. There's a risk here that we and AI may overlook or misinterpret minority traditions, leading to cultural homogenization.

We must address these biases to ensure AI serves as a tool for preservation rather than extinction.

There's no doubt that AI has reshaped the way we do business and impacted economies worldwide – the effects being positive and negative. On one hand, automation is replacing many manual jobs, displacing workers in factories and warehouses as AI-driven machinery increases efficiency.

On the other hand, AI has fueled economic growth in tech-savvy regions, creating high-skilled jobs in software development and data analysis.

This dual impact highlights the need for strategies that balance innovation with workforce inclusivity, ensuring opportunities still exist for those of us without advanced technical skills.

On the positive side, AI is bridging socioeconomic gaps and democratizing education by providing affordable and accessible personalized resources regardless of geography or income.

Healthcare professionals and patients around the world now have more medical information at their fingertips thanks to advances in AI. Doctors can now more easily diagnose rare diseases and make more informed decisions about treatments with the ability to analyze large volumes of patient data. In this sense, access to AI has extended essential medical services to those who might otherwise lack access, fostering a more equitable society.

Agriculture in developing countries is also benefitting from using AI to boost productivity by giving farmers the ability to more accurately predict weather patterns and crop yields as well as supporting food security. AI's multilingual abilities are also fostering better communication across local and regional cultures.

Moment of Reflection: Whose Voice Does AI Reflect?

Next time you use an AI tool such as a chatbot or a translation app, ask yourself whose perspective is shaping responses.

- Does it reflect diverse cultures and viewpoints, or does it feel one-sided?
- If something feels missing, what would you add to make it more inclusive?

Take a moment to notice how well AI represents *your* world.

10

GIVE YOUR CAREER A BOOST WITH AI BY YOUR SIDE

Today's job market has changed so much with our increasing reliance on AI, so the key to staying ahead is our ability to adapt and grow with these changes as new frontiers in career opportunities unfold. With so many AI-powered resources available to businesses and individuals, working from home and freelancing have become normal, and it's a trend that will continue to grow, so let's talk about how AI can help you upskill and evolve your role in the global workforce.

Upskill with AI for Career Growth

You no longer need in-depth technical knowledge to excel in the digital world of work and careers. If you already have a passion or skill that you want to develop into a money-making endeavor, you can start capitalizing on it by focusing on learning how to use AI tools effectively. Whatever business you're in, learning to work alongside AI will give you a competitive edge by improving decision-making, streamlining tasks, and personalizing customer experiences.

Gaining AI-powered data insights is one of the most valuable assets in industries such as marketing, where you can use AI to analyze customer trends and refine strategies to boost engagement.

In the field of finance, you can use AI-generated risk assessments to gain deeper market insights, and in HR, you can leverage AI-driven hiring tools to quickly identify top candidates. In these areas, the most important skill you can acquire is the ability to interpret AI-generated reports, recognize trends, and apply those insights.

Almost any industry you can imagine is benefitting from access to AI. Early adopters in sectors such as supply chain management, customer services, law and education – to name just a few – are now streaks ahead of slow-uptake competitors in terms of productivity and cost savings.

Even in administrative roles, AI can help you automate tasks and manage scheduling to improve efficiency and free up time for higher-value work.

Again, I must stress that employing critical thinking is equally important to ensure you're not totally dependent on AI for making important decisions. You still have to be acutely aware of the biases or inaccuracies that can arise if we just blindly follow AI recommendations. Use it as a supportive tool rather than a decision-maker.

Developing responsible AI usage can be a key career differentiator, but adopting this tech is all about improving all-round collaboration too, allowing project teams to work in the cloud and stay on task with management tools that foster transparency and accountability.

Being able to hire a team of specialists in their fields from diverse locations around the world has greatly contributed to breaking down cultural and ethical barriers. When you can literally watch work in progress from afar and see the big picture down to the finest detail as teams work together in the cloud, we are participating in evolving an equitable and ethical workspace.

Learning how AI works is also becoming more common and important in the workplace, so anything you can do to increase your knowledge and experience with AI tools will contribute to your career growth.

If you are new to AI assisted workspaces, start by experimenting with basic conversational tools such as ChatGPT as a sounding board, or one of the many user-friendly AI tools for boosting productivity such as Trello, or Notion AI. They'll give you an easy introduction to AI tools and you'll soon become more literate in the language surrounding them.

Moment of Reflection: Assess Your AI Skills

Take a moment to reflect on your current skill set and think about areas where AI can enhance your workflow and career in general.

What areas would benefit from AI-driven learning or tools?

When you've identified specific skills or competencies you wish to develop, explore AI platforms offering relevant courses or resources. Many are completely free, or you can sign up for a free trial.

Bring AI into Your Daily Workflow

Thinking about AI integration in your daily work is a great first step to start saving time by making routine tasks less burdensome.

With some of the task management tools mentioned earlier, you can share projects and set tasks for yourself and others on your team. The AI-enhanced tools help everyone on the team manage resources more efficiently, allocate tasks precisely, and predict project timelines accurately – resulting in smoother operations and fewer delays.

Test AI on a small scale first, such as using an AI-powered email filter or automatic report summaries, so you can evaluate its impact before full integration.

Remember, the goal is enhancement of your workflow by streamlining time-consuming tasks, not a replacement for your skills and knowledge. You may face common hurdles such as compatibility. As mentioned earlier, check the privacy settings of any apps or platforms you try. Over time, AI can become a trusted partner in optimizing your work and helping you focus on what truly matters. With this understanding, you're ready to embrace AI as a valuable tool in your professional journey.

Moment of Reflection: Spot AI Opportunities in Your Workflow

To identify where AI could make a difference to your daily work processes follow these steps:

1. Think of three repetitive and time consuming tasks that slow you down.
2. Pick one and find an AI tool that could help. It could be an email organizer, a task automation tool, or an AI assistant.
3. Try it out. Test the AI tool and see how it changes your workflow.

Reflect:

- Did it save you time?
- Did it improve efficiency?

- Would you keep using it?

Start small, experiment, and refine as you go. You'll soon see AI as a powerful partner in making your workday more efficient. If you're experimenting in the workplace, just be sure to check and follow any company policies regarding AI use and installing software, keeping in mind the ethics and responsibility that go with it.

How to Evolve Your Leadership Role with AI

Today's corporate leaders are capitalizing on the insights they get from AI for better decision making and keeping their teams up to speed in the digital age.

If you are in a leadership role and want to evolve with the times, adopting AI-driven solutions will give you new insights with functions such as predictive analytics to interpret complex data and translate it into actionable strategies.

But even if you're on board with initiating a digital transformation to work more transparently and efficiently, you could well face resistance from team members, which you'll have to address in order to progress.

Resistance to change is a common human trait that you are likely to encounter from some members of a team that are used to doing things the traditional way. Such resistance is often rooted in fear of the unknown or a disruption to routine. Pushback could also be because of the perceived threat that moving to digital management methods could replace human team members.

In situations like this, your role as a leader is to foster a culture of innovation as you guide team members through the transition, allaying their fears by showing how they'll be supported rather than replaced.

Developing an AI integration strategy that sets realistic objectives and supports broader business strategies will smooth the way and help you encourage team members to get on board with your organizational goals.

Beyond the technical aspects, you might need to employ some emotional intelligence to foster team cohesion and productivity. Demonstrating empathy and active listening will help you create an inclusive environment where team members feel valued and motivated. If you encourage continuous learning to ensure employees embrace AI, once they experience for themselves how much easier their jobs become, they'll see AI as a handy tool that enhances their job rather than replacing their abilities.

Demonstrating ethical leadership is central to building trust among stakeholders and successfully implementing AI in the workplace. Therefore, you must ensure that the AI you introduce actively promotes fairness, equality and equity.

Thankfully, AI excels at providing transparency for informed decision making, if you actively work to eliminate biases in any AI models that you use.

As you develop an ethical leadership strategy alongside your AI integration, it's an opportunity to consider the long-term societal impacts of using AI so you can make decisions that align with ethical standards and values. Instilling a strong ethical culture ultimately helps you navigate some of the complexities of AI with integrity and foresight, which you can easily achieve with a few AI-driven workshops and brainstorming sessions, encouraging teams to explore and experiment with AI applications.

Demonstrating the benefits of cross-disciplinary collaboration is another key strategy for encouraging others to adopt AI-driven technology. Your colleagues will soon see that bringing together diverse perspectives is beneficial to individuals and the team as a whole.

If you can champion innovation, you'll create an environment where AI thrives, driving progress and building a competitive advantage.

Moment of Reflection: Are You Ready to Lead in the AI Era?

Take a moment to reflect on your leadership approach in an AI-driven world:

- Do you trust AI to support your decisions, or do you feel unsure about relying on it?
- How do you typically react to AI-driven changes; excited, hesitant, or resistant?
- What's one way you can start using AI to help your team work smarter?

Based on your answers, choose one small step you can take to become more confident in leading with AI. It could be learning more, experimenting with AI tools, or encouraging your team to explore AI together. Every step forward brings you closer to your productivity goals.

Empowering Freelancers

If you're jumping out of the corporate world and going it alone as a freelancer, incorporating AI will make that leap of faith a lot more comforting.

Whatever your area of expertise, you can turn it into a viable freelancing gig with the flexibility and time-saving features AI-powered tools give you.

Whether your skills are in digital marketing, content creation, or any kind of creative endeavor, some of the AI tools we've discussed in this book will be instrumental in helping your freelance career take off.

In digital marketing, predictive analysis and anticipating marketing trends will give you data-driven insight. In content creation, AI will help you with inspiration and time-saving tricks such as crafting social media posts and email templates.

And even if you are freelancing, any collaborative projects you work on are likely to demand that you adopt whatever project management tools the team uses. So, in that respect, you must be open to embracing the AI technology they already use.

As a freelancer, you'll also have to keep track of finances yourself, and there are many AI tools that are specifically designed to do that for you, making it easy to collect payments, issue invoices and manage your bookkeeping proficiently with built-in security features too.

Freelancers can also attract more business by advertising that they provide superior services because they have AI tools as partners in their enterprise to ensure speedy and professional results.

A portfolio of satisfied clients, testimonials, and case studies should be part of your advertising arsenal that will help set you apart from competitors.

Moment of Reflection: Embracing AI in Your Freelance Journey

Take a moment to think about how AI could benefit your freelance business. Explore one AI tool that fits your niche and assess how it might help you in the following ways:

- How could it improve your processes or services?
- How would you explain these benefits to clients?
- Now, given your current understanding of AI, what's one step you can take today to start integrating it into your work?

Staying ahead of the curve is key, and this could be your first step toward ensuring you don't fall behind as the industry evolves.

PART IV: WHAT'S NEXT?

11

FUTURE TRENDS AND INNOVATIONS IN AI

AI is accelerating at an unprecedented pace with breakthroughs that are reshaping industries, redefining careers, and introducing possibilities that were previously unimaginable. In this chapter, let's look ahead at the trends shaping the future.

The Future of Work in an AI-Driven World

There's no doubt that AI and connectivity have already changed the way we work, and with it come fears of job displacement, especially in the labor sector, where AI can sometimes automate tasks once done manually. However, the impacts of AI on the world's workforce and on national economies is a really mixed bag of pros and cons that cannot easily be defined with a predictable figure.

Change is inevitable in any workplace, which has been evolving continually since the Industrial Revolution in the 18th century. Machines didn't necessarily replace people then. They just increased productivity beyond what was possible with manual labor alone. You still needed people overseeing the machines and taking care of all the other aspects of trade that machines weren't capable of.

The same is true today. Yes, we can expect to see many more changes over the next few decades, and yes, AI will impact people and economies in varying ways. The best we can do is be ready to embrace those changes and go with the flow in order to keep up with the inevitable changes to come.

The true impact of AI's evolving role in workplaces is anyone's guess. Nothing is set in stone. The International Monetary Fund, for example, predicted that AI will contribute to an increase in global GDP by $7 trillion or seven percent over the next 10 years, whereas Goldman Sachs predicted annual growth of between $17 and $25 trillion.

However, in a 2024 report published by Massachusetts Institute of Technology (MIT) titled *The Simple Macroeconomics of AI*, the author, Professor Daron Acemoglu, downplayed those claims. His prediction is a much more conservative estimate that GDPs will grow by only one percent in 10 years.

The report concluded that nearly 20 percent of all tasks in the US labor market could be replaced or augmented by AI but that only about a quarter of those tasks could be performed profitably by AI.

Nevertheless, job roles will certainly continue to change with AI doing more to assist in diverse areas of the world's workforce, but we should see it as a collaborative force assisting professionals with decision-making, workflow management, and performance optimization. As AI continues to evolve, individuals, organizations, and policymakers must navigate these changes thoughtfully to ensure that the future of work prioritizes human ingenuity, adaptability, and collaboration.

Countries investing in AI training, ethical AI regulation, and labor market adaptation will be best positioned to thrive, giving rise to two key questions:

- How should labor laws evolve to protect workers in an AI-powered job market?
- How can education systems prepare students for future jobs that don't yet exist?

The answers will shape the future of companies and countries, determining whether AI is a force for opportunity or disruption.

This doesn't mean that future workforces are divided into 'AI users' and 'AI developers'. It means that professionals must understand how to work alongside AI tools, adapt workflows, and apply critical thinking to AI insights.

Embracing AI does not require becoming a data scientist. It means understanding how AI fits into your profession and how to maximize its benefits.

The real challenge isn't whether AI will take over jobs, but whether we are prepared to evolve alongside it, ensuring creativity, ethics, and adaptability remain at the heart of an AI-driven workforce.

Moment of Reflection: AI Time Capsule – Your Job in 10 Years

Suppose it's 10 years from now, and AI has transformed your profession. Take a moment to consider the following:

- How has your role evolved with AI?
- What new skills have become essential?
- What surprised you most about the impact of AI?
- What challenges or opportunities emerged?

Now check how your vision of the future compares to what AI itself predicts by putting the question to ChatGPT like this:

"It's the year [10 years into the future], *and I work as* [your profession]. *Here's how I imagine my job has evolved with AI:* [paste your vision]. *Based on AI trends, how realistic is this? What else might I expect?"*

- Does AI confirm your predictions, or does it challenge your assumptions?
- What new possibilities does it reveal?

Adapting to the Rise of AI-Driven Industries

Almost every industry imaginable is undergoing a transformation with AI at the forefront of innovation. To thrive in this AI-driven world, you must have an understanding of how AI is reshaping industries, and which skills you should have so that you're comfortable working with AI. Let's look at how AI is being adopted in some of the world's major industries.

In agriculture, AI-powered precision farming is optimizing food production to make it more sustainable by giving farmers the ability to analyze real-time data on factors such as soil conditions, weather, and crop health. With AI-equipped drones, farmers can survey fields to optimize irrigation, fertilization, and find the best ways to use natural resources.

The way we harness natural resources for renewable energy is another area where AI is literally changing the landscape. As the shift toward clean energy accelerates, AI will continue to make renewable energy systems more efficient with AI-driven algorithms improving grid management, ensuring energy is distributed efficiently.

The retail sector will continue to evolve to offer consumers more personalized recommendations while benefiting from customer data analytics to optimize inventory. And, in manufacturing, the predictive abilities of AI can prevent machine failures, reducing downtime and improving efficiency.

As AI becomes further ingrained in industries, gaining data literacy is a valuable skill to have, so you can understand and act on the wealth of information available at our fingertips.

Computational thinking is equally important. Breaking down complex problems into manageable steps helps implement AI-driven solutions. Thinking algorithmically allows professionals to tackle challenges when integrating AI into workflows, improving customer experiences and operational efficiency.

As AI becomes more integrated in professional and social contexts, we'll also have to integrate more ethical decision making to ensure AI is used responsibly and the benefits are shared across society.

Moment of Reflection: Adapting to AI in Your Industry

Take a moment to reflect on how AI is impacting your industry:

- Do you recognize how AI is already changing your industry?
- How do you feel about these changes?
- How can AI help address key challenges in your industry?

Reflecting on these questions will help you better understand the current and future role of AI in your industry, and guide you to position yourself for success in an increasingly AI-driven world.

Innovations Shaping the Future of AI

A future where machines think more like humans, mimicking how our brains process information, is the vision behind 'neuromorphic computing'; a technology aimed at creating General AI with human-like cognition.

Neuromorphic computing is expected to be achieved by designing chips that simulate neural networks, which would enhance AI's adaptability and efficiency, moving beyond the task-specific nature of Narrow AI.

These systems could revolutionize fields requiring complex pattern recognition and decision-making, enabling intuitive human-machine interactions.

This could mean having robots that not only follow instructions but also understand context and nuance, making them truly collaborative tools in fields ranging from healthcare to customer service.

AI-powered robotics in manufacturing is equally transformative. Robots will learn and adapt in real time, reshaping production as they collaborate seamlessly with human workers to handle complex tasks. Again, this doesn't mean factory workers are going to be replaced. The human workforce will instead enjoy being able to focus more on strategy and quality control – ultimately making factory production more efficient.

We've already seen major advancements in autonomous vehicles (AVs) with high-resolution Light Detection and Ranging (LiDAR) to enhance environmental perception with remarkable accuracy.

Looking ahead, we may see hyper-autonomous vehicles capable of making decisions with minimal human input, integrating into smart cities. This transition will redefine urban mobility, offering safer, more efficient, and environmentally friendly travel solutions.

These advancements in AV technology are also expected to take space exploration to new heights with autonomous navigation that can make independent decisions, adapting to unforeseen challenges in deep space – a crucial factor for long-duration missions where communication delays prevent real-time Earth-based decision making.

A major breakthrough on the horizon in creative fields is the rapid advancement of 'generative adversarial networks' (GANs), which use two neural networks to create realistic outputs.

This technology already generates images, music, and text, but in the future, fully autonomous creative AI tools could design everything from art to architecture, opening new frontiers in digital creativity.

A marriage of AI with quantum computing is also expected to unlock exciting new possibilities with immense processing power at speeds unimaginable for conventional binary computers.

Quantum computing and AI combined could solve complex optimization problems, accelerate scientific discovery, and transform industries such as drug discovery, cryptography, and climate modeling.

As AI evolves, so will the vision of smart cities as AI integrates with the Internet of Things (IoT). By embedding sensors in urban infrastructure, AI will analyze real-time data to optimize everything from traffic flow to energy use and process it all in a centralized system.

Intelligent energy management such as street lighting based on pedestrian activity, as well as AI systems monitoring air quality and regulating pollution levels, are just some of the ways this AI-powered vision will make cities more sustainable, efficient, and livable.

Overall, AI-powered virtual assistants could evolve beyond functional tools by incorporating emotional intelligence into their functions. Hypothetically they'll respond to commands and have an understanding of human emotions and moods that allows them to react appropriately in different situations, creating more personalized and empathetic experiences that enhance daily life.

Moment of Reflection: Consider Your Role in the AI Future

Reflect on how these advancements might impact your life and the community in general as AI becomes more integrated into society.

- How might autonomous vehicles change your commute?
- How would AI diagnostics improve your healthcare experiences?
- What ethical considerations are most important?

Reflecting on these questions can help you understand your role in the AI-driven future and how you can contribute to it being adopted and developed responsibly.

12

STEP BEYOND LEARNING AI BASICS

Imagine walking into a library where the shelves are lined not with books but with endless rows of possibilities – each containing the potential to unlock new skills and understandings.

That's a simple analogy of how artificial intelligence offers a vast landscape of knowledge for those ready to explore beyond the basics.

Whether you're driven by curiosity or the desire to advance in your career, the journey into deeper AI learning is both challenging and rewarding. As with any field, the more you know, the more you can accomplish. Mastering the basics is just the beginning; the real adventure lies in discovering the specialized paths that AI offers the inquisitive.

Essential Online Resources for AI Mastery

Once you dive into using AI, keeping your skills relevant is essential to stay competitive and maximize its capabilities in personal and professional settings.

This book along with your free **AI Quick-Start Toolkit** should give you a good head start, and expanding your knowledge beyond the basics is a piece of cake with a growing number of online resources available to anyone who wants to reap the benefits that AI brings to business and leisure alike.

To brush up on using AI in business, AI-driven productivity, and ethical use of AI, you can try platforms such as Coursera and edX, which offer structured courses and give you industry insights without requiring you to have any technical expertise.

Also search for AI MOOCs (Massive Open Online Courses), which are free or low-cost AI courses from universities, tech companies, and educational platforms. They offer structured learning paths for beginners to explore practical applications without needing any technical expertise. There's a lot to choose from so just select courses that interest you so you can stay focused and make steady progress.

The University of Helsinki, for example, offers a free, beginner-friendly introductory course called 'Elements of AI' that helps you build confidence in using AI tools

Google's 'AI Essentials' program covers practical applications of generative AI and responsible AI usage, making it a solid choice for improving AI understanding without diving into programming.

If you prefer flexible, interactive learning, Superhuman AI offers courses for non-technical professionals, teaching AI integration for better productivity.

'AI For Everyone' by DeepLearning.AI is another great starting point if you want to understand the impact of AI in a professional setting and learn how to work with AI-powered tools.

Udacity is another good one for beginners, and gives a more immersive experience with expert courses too, as it focuses on practical AI applications in fields such as marketing, finance, and operations.

Google's AI certification and beginner-friendly courses such as 'Artificial Intelligence and Machine Learning Basics for Non-Technical Professionals' introduce key concepts without requiring coding experience. Learning data analysis, statistics, and Python can also be helpful stepping stones if you're interested in AI development.

You really don't need any coding skills to become an expert AI user, but if you do want to explore the technical side and get into AI development or want a deeper understanding, Coursera's 'Machine Learning Specialization' offers a strong foundation in machine learning applications.

The goal isn't to become an AI expert, but to be AI-savvy – leveraging AI tools to work smarter, innovate, and grow professionally.

Moment of Reflection: Jumpstart Your AI Journey

Pick an AI topic that excites you and find an online course or certification to explore it further. Many are free and offered by reputable organizations. Ask:

- What skills will you gain?
- How will it enhance your career or daily life?

Think of a hands-on way to apply your learning, then dive in and get started!

Find Your AI Community and Build Connections

If you want to chat with others in a similar position to yourself or want some tips and advice from experienced AI users, look for an online AI forum to join. They're excellent places to learn about the pros and cons of different AI tools from people that are usually more than happy to share their experiences. Whatever you're using AI for, you should be able to easily find a forum that suits your situation and level of expertise, even if you're still just dabbling.

If you're more interested in how AI can help you in business than the technical aspects, you can find groups for non-technical users on Facebook Groups and among LinkedIn communities.

On Reddit, find discussions about AI tools and trends at r/ArtificialIntelligence and r/ChatGPT.

For live interactions on the AI topic that you're interested in, try Discord and Slack communities, and if you're interested in joining AI networking events and workshops, have a look at Meetup.com.

Kaggle is a popular platform and online community for anyone interested in data science and machine learning. It's packed with tools and resources, so it's also a good place for beginners to sign up for a structured AI development course.

Building a network within these communities requires your active participation. Start by browsing discussions to see what topics people are engaging with. Many groups have beginner-friendly sections where you can ask simple questions such as 'What's a good AI tool for small businesses?' or 'How do you use AI for content creation?'.

Sharing your experiences with AI tools such as ChatGPT or Canva's AI features can spark valuable discussions. Your contributions help others while establishing your presence in the community. You'll find many others on these forums that are very willing to clarify things or give pointers. Over time, you'll connect with like-minded individuals, which could lead to exciting opportunities to collaborate, and will be valuable learning experiences.

As a beginner wanting to explore AI for workflow improvements, you might find a mentor among community members who can guide you and help you gain confidence.

Try It Yourself: Engage with an AI Community

Choose an AI community from the ones mentioned in this chapter and spend 10 to 15 minutes exploring it. Find a discussion that interests you then make a comment or ask a question in the forum.

Take note of any insights you get and see if there's anything to be gained that might help in your AI journey. Even small interactions can help you build confidence and connections.

- Did you get an answer to your question from another forum member?
- Was the response helpful?

Join AI Meetups and Study Groups

AI meetups and study groups are excellent opportunities to network with AI users and developers in person.

These kinds of gatherings aren't just for tech professionals. Whether you're a small business owner automating tasks, a content creator exploring AI tools, or just curious about AI's impact, meetups provide a space to learn, share experiences, and stay informed about advancements.

Some events focus on practical AI applications, offering demos on tools that streamline work and boost creativity. Others feature guest speakers discussing AI's role in industries such as marketing and healthcare.

With a quick search you can find groups including the non-profit 'Women in AI' group and the 'Data Science Group', which is the largest discussion community on this topic on Facebook.

Meetup.com and Eventbrite are great platforms to start looking for AI study groups. If there aren't any groups in your area, you could try starting one up yourself. Venues can be found by partnering with libraries, coworking spaces, or business groups. The goal isn't to be an expert. It's about learning together and exploring AI's potential in a way that fits your needs.

Try It Yourself: Make Your First Move

Take five minutes to search for an AI meetup or online study group near you. If you can't find one, think about starting your own – perhaps a casual AI discussion over coffee with a few peers.

- What topics interest you most?
- Jot down one question you'd love to ask at your first meetup.

The first step in growing with AI is simply showing up!

Keep Up with AI Trends and Opportunities

You can see how quickly AI has evolved over the past few years by comparing how easy it is these days to have complex conversations with voice assistants such as Siri and Alexa, compared to the limited ability they had to understand simple voice commands when they were first launched.

Staying informed about AI's rapid evolution isn't just about keeping up – it's about staying adaptable to ongoing change.

Following AI developments helps you anticipate industry shifts rather than react to them. This foresight allows you to seize opportunities, whether it's adopting new technology or aligning your career with emerging trends.

As we've seen, you'll find diverse views from news sources about the impact of AI so finding a source that you trust is important for getting impartial information. *The Verge* and *Wired* magazines are good at breaking down complex topics into accessible insights, dissecting the latest trends and predicting future directions, while TED Talks on AI offer compelling discussions from industry leaders.

Podcasts such as 'Hard Fork' provide engaging conversations on AI's role in society, business, and daily life as well.

To curate a personalized AI news feed, you can set up Google Alerts with keywords such as 'Generative AI in business', and you can subscribe to AI-focused newsletters such as 'Import AI', authored by Jack Clark, a prominent AI policy expert and former Policy Director at OpenAI, which provides concise summaries of key developments.

You can find more advanced AI trend reports from McKinsey and OpenAI, both of which offer valuable insights that'll help you anticipate changes before they go mainstream.

Of course nothing is more informative than having hands-on experience with AI tools, so do try experimenting with new applications. Whether testing a generative AI writing assistant, AI-driven analytics, or AI-generated content, having first-hand experience will give you an intrinsic understanding of AI's capabilities and limitations.

Moment of Reflection: How Will You Stay AI-Informed?

Take a moment to reflect on staying up to date with AI trends:

- If you had to explain one recent AI trend to a friend, what would it be?
- What's one simple habit you can adopt to stay updated on AI (reading one article a week, following an expert, testing new tools)?

Taking a small step today keeps you ahead tomorrow!

Keep the Game Alive

Thank you for reading *Generative AI for Beginners*! By reading this book, you now know how much AI is transforming the way we live, work, and create – and how our choices in using it will shape the future.

That's why your voice matters.

Please take a few moments to leave a review on Amazon.

You'll help others find this book and give them the confidence to see for themselves the benefits of bringing AI into their lives.

Sharing your thoughts – what you've learned, how AI is helping you, or what surprised you – can inspire others to begin their journey with the right mindset.

Just a few words from you could make a big difference!

If you're ready to help shape the future of AI, please leave a review here:

https://geni.us/euJNPNB

Thank you for being part of this rapidly evolving movement. As users, we have the power to make sure it moves in the right direction. Let's use it wisely to grow, create, and become a better version of ourselves, together.

Sarah T. Rowan

Conclusion

When we began this exploration, I shared my transition from AI skepticism to enthusiastic adoption. Now, having explored these tools together, I hope you've experienced a similar transformation in how you view AI's potential in your life.

By now, you should have a strong grasp of the foundational concepts plus a clear vision of how you can use AI to enhance your personal and professional endeavors.

Looking back, we've discovered the incredible potential of AI to streamline tasks, boost productivity, and unlock new avenues for creativity. From writing captivating stories with AI-powered tools to designing personalized meal plans and fitness routines, the possibilities are truly endless.

We've also tackled the ethical considerations surrounding AI, emphasizing the importance of fairness, transparency, and accountability in its development and deployment.

The practical applications we've explored throughout this book reflect my own experience integrating AI into different aspects of life. These tools have become indispensable – simplifying daily tasks, enhancing creative projects, supporting personal growth, and connecting me with a community of forward-thinkers who share a passion for building a better future in partnership with AI.

This same potential is now within your reach, harness it to transform your life.

Do keep in mind, though, that AI is not a magic wand that will solve all our problems. It is a tool that complements and enhances human capabilities, not a replacement for them.

When integrating AI into your daily life, use a balanced approach that leverages AI's strengths while relying on your own intuition and creativity. Embrace the opportunities AI presents, but also remain mindful of its limitations and the need for human oversight.

As you embark on this path, you're joining millions of professionals, creators, and problem-solvers who are excited about exploring AI's potential. By actively engaging in AI communities – sharing insights, asking questions, and experimenting with new tools – you contribute to AI's evolution. Your experiences help refine best practices, identify ethical concerns, and drive innovation. Your voice matters in shaping an AI-powered future that is responsible, ethical, and beneficial to all.

This final page marks not an ending, but just the beginning of your AI journey. The real value of this book lies not in reading it, but in applying it, and each small success will build confidence for the next step. The AI frontier is constantly advancing, and your willingness to experiment and learn will determine how much value you extract from these powerful tools.

While navigating this exciting landscape, remember to approach AI with an open mind, a critical eye, and a commitment to lifelong learning. Together, we can harness the potential of AI to create a future that is more efficient, creative, and inclusive.

The AI revolution is happening with or without us – but thanks to the practical insights from this book and your renovated awareness, you can now ensure it happens with you, shaped by your values and directed by your decisions as we collectively write the next chapter of human progress.

References

360Learning Blog. (n.d.). *The top 10 AI-powered learning platforms in 2025.* https://360learning.com/blog/ai-learning-platforms/

Acemoglu, D. (2024, May). *Macroeconomics of AI.* Massachusetts Institute of Technology (MIT). https://shapingwork.mit.edu/wp-content/uploads/2024/05/Acemoglu_Macroeconomics-of-AI_May-2024.pdf

Adam, F. (2024, July 3). *AI tools for beginners: A comprehensive guide.* Medium. https://medium.com/@fahmiadam/ai-tools-for-beginners-a-comprehensive-guide-0c71f4416d73

Adecco Group. (2024, October 17). *Adecco Group's 2024 Global Workforce of the Future Survey* [Press release]. https://www.adeccogroup.com/our-group/media/press-releases/ai-saves-workers-an-average-of-one-hour-each-day

Adobe. (2023, April 30). *Creativity with AI in Education 2025 Report.* https://acrobat.adobe.com/id/urn:aaid:sc:US:b18d23f9-f0c3-4b80-8018-14c46124b58f

Adobe. (2023, November 27). *Real-world AI image generator situations.* https://helpx.adobe.com/lv/express/how-to/ai-image-generator-workflows.html

AI-Pro. (2024, July 2). *The top AI resources for learning: Courses and online platforms.* https://ai-pro.org/learn-ai/articles/the-top-ai-resources-for-learning-courses-and-online-platforms/

Amara, S. (2024, October 1). *The ultimate guide to paid and free AI tools in 2024.* Medium. https://medium.com/@simohamed.amara/the-ultimate-guide-to-paid-and-free-ai-tools-in-2024-4b230c78e538

Amazon Web Services. (n.d.). *What's the difference between AI and machine learning?* https://aws.amazon.com/compare/the-difference-between-artificial-intelligence-and-machine-learning/

Anderson, J. (2025, January 8). *20 best AI language learning apps in 2025.* Makes You Fluent. https://makesyoufluent.com/ai-language-learning-apps/

Barley, A. (2024, October 31). *The rise of AI in mental health apps: Top 5 apps transforming mental health care.* The Dawn Rehab. https://thedawnrehab.com/blog/the-rise-of-ai-in-mental-health-top-5-apps-transforming-mental-health-care/

Bessalel, S. (2023, September 11). *LinkedIn Learning's 10 Most Popular AI Courses of the Year.* LinkedIn Business Learning Blog. https://www.linkedin.com/business/learning/blog/linkedin-learning-most-popular-ai-courses-of-the-year

Campbell, F. (n.d.). *The top 10 AI-powered learning platforms in 2025.* 360Learning Blog. https://360learning.com/blog/ai-learning-platforms/

Chase, N. (2025, February 3). *11+ best AI novel writing software tools in 2025.* Neil Chase Film. https://neilchasefilm.com/ai-novel-writing-software/

Codecademy Team. (n.d.). *AI prompting best practices*. Codecademy. https://www.codecademy.com/article/ai-prompting-best-practices

Dallas Artificial Intelligence and Deep Learning. (n.d.). Meetup. https://www.meetup.com/dallas-artificial-intelligence-deep-learning/

Dennison, K. (2023, March 14). *The impact of artificial intelligence on leadership: How to leverage AI to improve decision making*. Forbes. https://www.forbes.com/sites/karadennison/2023/03/14/the-impact-of-artificial-intelligence-on-leadership-how-to-leverage-ai-to-improve-decision-making/

Diaz, I. (2024, March 19). *Ethical considerations in AI development*. Apium Hub. https://apiumhub.com/tech-blog-barcelona/ethical-considerations-ai-development/

Digital Education Council. (2024, August 2). *Digital Education Council Global AI Student Survey 2024*. https://www.digitaleducationcouncil.com/post/digital-education-council-global-ai-student-survey-2024

Eden AI. (n.d.). *7 steps to adopting AI workflows in your business*. https://www.edenai.co/post/steps-to-adopting-ai-workflows-in-your-business

Ellis, E. (2023, October). *AI technology round-up: October 2023*. Content Cucumber. https://wordpress.contentcucumber.com/blog/ai-tech-round-up-october-2023/

Everfit Team. (2024, February 5). *AI in fitness coaching: A deep dive into real-world use cases*. Everfit Blog. http://blog.everfit.io/ai-in-fitness-coaching-a-deep-dive-into-real-world-use-cases

Gcore. (2023, April 30). *Best AI tools to step up content writing in 2023*. Gcore Blog. https://gcore.com/blog/best-ai-content-writing-tools-2023/

Gertenbach, E. (2024, October 24). *The 28 best AI tools for freelancers in 2025*. Upwork. https://www.upwork.com/resources/ai-tools-for-freelancers

Guinness, H. (2024, September 9). *The 6 best AI writing generators*. Zapier. https://zapier.com/blog/best-ai-writing-generator/

Guinness, H. (2024, September 9). *The top AI art generators*. Zapier. https://zapier.com/blog/ai-art-generator/

Hillier, W. (2024, January 12). *How to use ChatGPT: The full guide for beginners*. Careerfoundry. https://careerfoundry.com/en/blog/digital-marketing/how-to-use-chatgpt/

History of artificial intelligence. (n.d.). In Wikipedia. Retrieved February 20, 2025, from https://en.wikipedia.org/wiki/History_of_artificial_intelligence

Juneja, H. (2024, August 12). *AI in fitness app: Transforming the fitness industry with smart technology*. Wegile. https://wegile.com/insights/ai-in-fitness-app.php

Kelly, R. (2024, August 28). *Survey: 86% of students already use AI in their studies*. Campus Technology. https://campustechnology.com/articles/2024/08/28/survey-86-of-students-already-use-ai-in-their-studies.aspx

Lang, K. (2024, April 9). *8 of the best AI productivity tools to help you optimize how you work*. Buffer. https://buffer.com/resources/ai-productivity-tools/

Levis, M. (2024, January 16). *Understanding the limitations of AI (Artificial intelligence)*. Medium. https://medium.com/@marklevisebook/understanding-the-limitations-of-ai-artificial-intelligence-a264c1e0b8ab

Mahas, G. (2025, January 14). *AI in personal finance*. Innovation Strategy. https://www.innovationstrategy.com/article/ai-in-personal-finance

Mahnot, S. (2003, April 26). *How AI is revolutionizing personal development: The next big thing!* The Blog Relay. https://theblogrelay.com/how-ai-is-revolutionizing-personal-development-the-next-big-thing/

Marr, B. (2023, July 5). *Debunking AI myths: The truth behind 5 common misconceptions*. Forbes. https://www.forbes.com/sites/bernardmarr/2023/07/05/debunking-ai-myths-the-truth-behind-5-common-misconceptions/

Marr, B. (2024, April 18). *The role of generative AI in video game development*. Forbes. https://www.forbes.com/sites/bernardmarr/2024/04/18/the-role-of-generative-ai-in-video-game-development/

Martin, B. (n.d.). *The 9 best AI courses online for 2025: Beginner to advanced*. LearnDataSci. https://www.learndatasci.com/best-artificial-intelligence-ai-courses/

Mucci, T. (2024, April 18). *Getting ready for artificial general intelligence with examples*. IBM. https://www.ibm.com/think/topics/artificial-general-intelligence-examples

Natasha. (2023, April 13). *Top AI communities in 2023*. AI Vanguard. https://medium.com/ai-vanguard/top-ai-communities-in-2023-403254cb05f1

National Institute of Standards and Technology. (n.d.). *3 AI Risks and Trustworthiness*. AI Resource Center Knowledge Base. https://airc.nist.gov/AI_RMF_Knowledge_Base/AI_RMF/Foundational_Information/3-sec-characteristics

Needhi, J. (2024, May 28). *Autonomous vehicles 2030 and beyond: Recent advances and future trends.* Medium. https://medium.com/@jeyadev_needhi/autonomous-vehicles-2030-and-beyond-recent-advances-and-future-trends-d4969e731b81

Noble Desktop. (n.d.). *The role of feedback in developing better generative AI models.* https://www.nobledesktop.com/learn/ai/the-role-of-feedback-in-developing-better-generative-ai-models

O'Brien, K. (2024, October 15). *Upskilling and reskilling for talent transformation in the era of AI.* IBM. https://www.ibm.com/think/insights/ai-upskilling

O'Toole, K., et al. (2024, August). *Extending human creativity with AI.* Science Direct. https://www.sciencedirect.com/science/article/pii/S2713374524000062

Oza, H. (2024, February 8). *The role of artificial intelligence in smart home systems.* Hdata Systems. https://www.hdatasystems.com/blog/the-role-of-ai-in-smart-home-systems

Pappu, N. (n.d.). *AI ethics 101: Comparing IEEE, EU and OECD guidelines.* Zendata. https://www.zendata.dev/post/ai-ethics-101

Pazzanese, C. (2020, October 26). *Great promise but potential for peril.* The Harvard Gazette. https://news.harvard.edu/gazette/story/2020/10/ethical-concerns-mount-as-ai-takes-bigger-decision-making-role/

Personal AI. (2024, November). *Customizing your AI.* https://product-docs.personal.ai/customizing-your-ai

PR Newswire. (2023, October 2). *The Yummly app introduces 3 new features to simplify mealtime inspiration & planning.* https://www.prnewswire.com/news-releases/the-yummly-app-introduce

s-3-new-features-to-simplify-mealtime-inspiration--planning-301943590.html

PwC Global. (n.d.). *PwC's global artificial intelligence study: Sizing the prize.* https://www.pwc.com/gx/en/issues/artificial-intelligence/publications/artificial-intelligence-study.html

Shah, H. (2024, October 21). *AI in mobile phones: How AI is revolutionizing smartphones.* Prismetric. https://www.prismetric.com/ai-in-mobile-phones/

Shah, P. F. (n.d.). *Top 10 Gen AI travel planning apps, tools, and assistants.* Ahoy Matey Blog. https://www.ahoymatey.blog/gen-ai-travel-planning-apps/

Shelf. (n.d.). *AI glossary: 80 essential artificial intelligence terms explained*. https://shelf.io/ai-glossary/

Tableau. (n.d.). *14 of the best books about artificial intelligence (AI) for any level.* https://www.tableau.com/learn/articles/books-about-artificial-intelligence

The Label Machine. (n.d.). *Music AI tools Master List.* The Label Machine Blog. https://thelabelmachine.com/blog/music-ai-tools-list/

Umadevi, R. (2024, October 1). *Three key prompting frameworks: RTF, TAG, and RACEF.* Medium. https://medium.com/@poojaauma/3-key-prompting-frameworks-rtf-tag-and-racef-e701e95aae2b

University of Minnesota, Carlson School of Management. (2024, May 17). *Debunking 5 artificial intelligence myths.* https://carlsonschool.umn.edu/graduate/resources/debunking-5-artificial-intelligence-myths

Vicente, L., et al. (2023, October 3). *Humans inherit artificial intelligence biases*. Scientific Reports. https://www.nature.com/articles/s41598-023-42384-8

Vicente, L., et al. (2024, July 18). *Protecting data privacy as a baseline for responsible AI*. Center for Strategic & International Studies. https://www.csis.org/analysis/protecting-data-privacy-baseline-responsible-ai

Walch, K. (2024, August 16). *How AI is revolutionizing professional sports*. Forbes. https://www.forbes.com/sites/kathleenwalch/2024/08/16/how-ai-is-revolutionizing-professional-sports/

Whitworth, M., et al. (2024, September 10). *Artificial intelligence and quantum computing*. S&P Global. https://www.spglobal.com/en/research-insights/special-reports/artificial-intelligence-and-quantum-computing-the-fundamentals